Blessed Are the Hungry

Blessed Are the Hungry

Meditations on the Lord's Supper

Peter J. Leithart

Canon Press
MOSCOW • IDAHO

Peter J. Leithart, *Blessed are the Hungry: Meditations on the Lord's Supper*

© 2000 by Peter J. Leithart
Published by Canon Press, P.O. Box 8729, Moscow, ID 83843
800-488-2034 / www.canonpress.org

01 00 99 98 97   9 8 7 6 5 4 3 2 1

Cover design by Paige Atwood Design, Moscow, ID
Printed in the United States of America.

The closing essay, "The Way Things Really Ought To Be: Eucharist, Eschatology, and Culture" was first published in the *Westminster Theological Journal*, 59 (1997).

Library of Congress Cataloging-in-Publication Data

    Leithart, Peter J.
        Blessed are the hungry / Peter J. Leithart.
        p. cm.
        Includes index.
        ISBN 1–885767–73–0 (pbk.)
        1. Lord's Supper—Meditations. I. Title.
        BV825.2 .L45 2000
        264'.36—dc21   00–010484

To Jordan

μακάριοι οἱ πεινῶντες
νῦν ὅτι χορτασθήσεσθε

TABLE OF CONTENTS

Acknowledgments

This small volume is the fruit of over a decade of reflection and meditation on and, most importantly, celebration of the Lord's Supper. I began to consider writing such a book while I was serving as pastor of Reformed Heritage Presbyterian Church in Birmingham, Alabama (1989–1995). For several years, we celebrated the Lord's Supper every week, and I made an effort at the end of every sermon to say a few words to connect the sermon topic to the meal. I discovered that, without stretching things, the Supper could be brought to bear on everything I said from the pulpit, and this led to the conclusion briefly articulated in the introduction, that the Supper's significance is as broad as the creation itself.

Cindy Douglas especially encouraged me to write these meditations and publish them. I hope she is satisfied with the results.

Though my doctoral work at Cambridge dealt specifically with baptism, it involved some study of sacramental theology in general and the Lord's Supper. In the course of those studies, I was continually encouraged and stimulated by conversations with my doctoral supervisor, John Milbank, and am grateful to him.

As usual, I owe enormous intellectual debts to James B. Jordan. In particular, his wonderful series of essays on "food and faith" provided a good deal of stimulation for this book, and many of the points in chapter 17 came from a draft of his forthcoming commentary on Daniel.

Thanks to Doug Jones of Canon Press, for his interest in the book and his gentle encouragement to finish it in a timely fashion.

Holly McBroom (soon-to-be-McCabe) worked steadily to correct the manuscript during her last weeks at Canon Press. I have inexcusably failed to acknowledge Holly's work on my previous books, and, though this brief and belated thanks cannot make up for past oversights, at least I hope it is an indication of my gratitude for her carefulness and enthusiasm.

I have dedicated each of my last several books to one of my children, working in succession from the oldest down the list. Jordan, my second son, was next on the list. But it is one of those delightful serendipities of life that *Blessed Are the Hungry* should be dedicated to him, for Jordan is a hungry young man, not only in the obvious sense that all fourteen-year-old boys are hungry but also in his passion to live, to know, and to win. May he always be filled with the living Bread, which gives life.

Introduction

The Lord's Supper is the world in miniature; it has cosmic significance. Within it we find clues to the meaning of all creation and all history, to the nature of God and the nature of man, to the mystery of the world, which is Christ. It is not confined to the first day, for its power fills seven. Though the table stands at the center, its effects stretch out to the four corners of the earth.

This book is written on the assumption that the assertions in the previous paragraph are true. It is not a defense of these assertions, except in the roundabout sense captured by that axiom about proofs and puddings. It is instead a collection of more or less discrete (and somewhat repetitive) meditations on Scripture passages that shed some light on the meaning of the Supper. It is not a comprehensive book in any sense, but rather a very selective and hopefully suggestive sampling. My goal here is to gesture toward the boundaries of the Supper's significance; it is not my purpose to provide a survey map of the whole territory. With these things in mind, I imagine it would be best not to read all the essays in one sitting. The book would work best if each chapter were read individually, perhaps as preparation for communion.

Though designed as meditations, they are also intended as a small contribution to more technical discussions of sacramental theology. For centuries, theologians have attempted to explain "what happens in holy communion" by employing philosophical concepts—derived from Aristotelian or existential-personalist or some other philosophical tradition—or, more recently, by using models from the social sciences. In many ways, these efforts (framed in what theologians call "second order discourse") have been illuminating and have contributed to a fuller practice of the Supper. But such efforts give the illusion of moving beyond the "naive" outlook of Scripture to the more "fundamental" reality of the sacrament. I have written out of the contrary conviction that the Scriptural descriptions of the Supper are the most fundamental possible descriptions, though they may be elaborated (carefully) using extra-biblical concepts. To the question, "What happens in holy communion?" my first answer is thus not "The whole substance of the bread and wine is changed into the substance of the body and blood of Jesus"; nor "We enter into the divine present where the past event of Jesus' death is eternally re-presented"; nor "We have a personal encounter with the risen Christ through the medium of signs"; nor "We move ritually through a liminal moment of *communitas* toward the renewal of differentiated community." Some of these expressions are, I believe, simply wrong, but even if they were all perfectly correct, they would get us no closer to the base reality of the Supper than the variety of biblical descriptions.

What happens in holy communion? I wish to say: "We, as children of Adam, are offered the trees of the garden; as sons of Abraham, we celebrate a victory feast in the King's Valley; as holy ones, we receive holy food; as the true Israel, we feed on the land of milk and honey; as exiles returned to Zion, we eat marrow and fat, and drink wine on the lees; we who are many are made one loaf, and commune with the body and blood of Christ; we are the bride celebrating the marriage supper of the Lamb, and we are also the bride undergoing the test of jealousy; at the Lord's table we commit ourselves to shun the table of demons." This book offers no proof that a typological framework for sacramental theology is as rich and, in its way, as precise and technical as a philosophical framework, but I hope it will at least make that claim plausible. Proofs and puddings, again.

I am not avoiding defense because my assertions are indefensible. I have included a closing essay that comes closer to defending my assumptions in a rigorous way (though even that moves in a rather impressionistic direction), and I hope someday to write a more systematic theology of the sacraments. For those who find the assertions of the first paragraph striking or simply odd, however, a brief discussion would be helpful.

The claims made in the first paragraph above may be defended from two angles, one soteriological, the other eschatological. The soteriological argument is this: At the heart of our redemption is our union with Christ in His death, resurrection, and ascension. We are justified by union with Christ's resurrection, adopted in the Son, made alive together with the One whom the Father raised from the dead, sanctified by the indwelling presence of Christ through His Spirit, made priests and kings in the Priest and King. In whatever way we wish to describe our redemption, we are describing some aspect of our union with Christ (see, further, chapter twenty-seven).

And this is precisely the soteriological meaning of the Lord's Supper: "Is not the cup, which we bless, a communion in the blood of Christ? Is not the bread, which we break, a communion in the body of Christ?" (1 Corinthians 10:16). If these two things are true—that union with Christ is the fundamental reality of our salvation and that the Supper is communion with Christ—then the Supper must mean everything that union with Christ means. The Supper is a ritual sign of our justification, for in it God shows that He considers us righteous, i.e., table fellows and covenant-keepers; it is a sign of our adoption, for we are given food by our heavenly Father; through bread and wine we are joined to the power of the risen Christ, who is present in and through His Spirit; in the Supper we are raised to heaven to feast on Christ, enthroned in heavenly places, admitted to the holy place to eat sacred bread. The significance of the Supper is as high and deep and wide as salvation itself.

Further, Jesus is the climax and recapitulation of all redemptive history. He is the victorious Seed promised outside the gates of Eden, the miracle Child of Abraham, the true Israel, the Prophet greater than Moses, the Priest after the order of Melchizedek, great David's greater Son. The whole history of Scripture is the history of Christ Jesus, and in the Supper we are inserted into this Christ and this history. Redemptive history came to a climax when the Father sent the Son who gave Himself as the bread from heaven, for the life of the world. Therefore, the meal in which we feed on Christ is the climax of salvation history. To put it yet another way, the Bible is about the *totus Christus*, the whole Christ, Head and Body. Since the body of Christ is formed as body at the table, the whole Bible is about this meal.

The eschatological argument is this: Scripture teaches that the final order of things will be the kingdom of God, and Jesus consistently described the kingdom of God as a place of feasting. Better, the kingdom is not a place where feasting occurs, but the feast itself. The trajectory of human history was set at the cross, and it has been set to this one end: That the elect may feast forever in the presence of God. At the Lord's table, we receive an initial taste of the final heavens and earth, but the Lord's Supper is not merely a *sign* of the eschatological feast, as if the two were separate feasts. Instead, the Supper is the early stage of that very feast. Every time we celebrate the Lord's Supper, we are displaying in history a glimpse of the end of history and anticipating in this world the order of the world to come. Our feast is not the initial form of one small part of the new creation; it is the initial form of the new creation itself. And this means that the feast that we already enjoy is as wide in scope as the feast that we will enjoy in the new creation. That is to say, it is as wide as creation itself (see, further, the closing essay).

Therefore, Lord's Supper is the world in miniature; it has cosmic significance. Within it we find clues to the meaning of all creation and all history, to the nature of God and the nature of man, to the mystery of the world, which is Christ. It is not confined to the first day, for its power fills seven. Though the table stands at the center, its effects stretch out to the four corners of the earth.

Appropriately enough, I am completing work on this book on Ascension Day, year 2000 of the reign of Jesus. My hope is that it might enable Christians to see more clearly not just the connection but the identity of the twin confession of the church: That Jesus is Lord of His table and that He is Lord of all.

Peniel Hall
Ascension Day 2000

I
Love Made Food

Then God said, 'Behold, I have given you every plant yielding seed that is on the face of all the earth, and every tree which has fruit yielding seed, it shall be food for you' (Genesis 1:29).

Marduk had a problem. He had been acclaimed as chief of the gods after crushing the skull of Tiamat, who was the closest thing he had to a mother. In the heavens, he had set up stations for the gods and their constellations, and formed the moon to keep track of days and months. But the gods were still not satisfied. They were hungry and demanded relief. So Marduk presented a plan to his fellow deities:

> Blood I will mass and cause bones to be.
> I will establish a savage, "man" shall be his
>   name.
> Verily, savage man I will create.
> He shall be charged with the service of the gods
> That they might be at ease.

Formed from the blood of the rebel god Kingu, Marduk made man to "establish for his fathers the great food offerings," to bear "food-offerings . . . for their gods and goddesses."

In the margin to E. A. Speiser's translation of this Akkadian myth, known as the *Enuma Elish*, there is a cross reference to Genesis 1:26 ("Let us make man as Our image, after Our likeness"). No doubt there are shadowy parallels between the two creation accounts, but the differences could hardly be starker, particularly regarding the role of food in the two stories. For the Akkadians, man exists to feed the gods; in the Bible, God creates man and then offers *him* food. In fact, God's gift of food is the climax of the six days of creation. Day six does not end with man's creation as the image of God or with God's command that Adam rule the earth, its oxen and its beasts. Genesis 1 ends, rather, with a menu.

The radical difference between the Creator and all idols is evident here: idols demand a *quid pro quo* and enter into the human cycle of exchange because they have needs and desires that humans can meet, whether for bread or affirmation or pleasure. Since they are creatures falsely treated as gods, idols cannot help being just as dependent as all other creatures are. Precisely because He is Creator, however, the living God needs nothing that He has made, and creatures can never offer a sufficient *quid* for His *quo*. Everything that creatures have, including our very existence, is a gift of sheer grace, an overflow of the self-giving love that is God's eternal character. Like Marduk, Yahweh ends His creative work by setting a table. Quite unlike Marduk, who wants to secure his own portion, Yahweh sets His table for man.

Food reveals not only the nature of God but the creaturely nature of God's image. Even the smallest infant knows instinctively that food is life, and the creation account shows that even unfallen Adam had to eat. But this commonsensical equation of food and life is only part of the truth. Calvin understood that Jesus was being quite literal when He said, "Man does not live by bread alone." How, after all, can food, which is dead, give life? Such a "resurrection" cannot be explained by any natural process but is possible only for the One who calls things that are not as though they were. Nourishment is a miracle, similar to the sacrificial miracle by which the seed must die in order to produce fruit. By its very deadness, food discloses that, beyond our dependence on food, our life is completely dependent on the Word that proceeds from the mouth of God.

Adam's menu discloses the secret of human beings in another sense as well. Influenced by Greek and Enlightenment perspectives, modern Christians assume that ideas and thoughts and other functions of reason are superior to the body and its desires. For nearly two millennia, theologians have claimed that the image of God is located primarily if not exclusively in rationality or mental capacities. In no way do I wish to minimize the wonder of the human mind, whose measureless corridors reflect the incomprehensible God. But there is nothing at all said about the brain or thinking in Genesis 1, nothing that suggests that silent contemplation is more fully human than eating a good meal. Quite the contrary: when God spoke to Adam, He did not reveal the Pythagorean theorem or teach the intricacies of superstring theory; He offered food. Adam did not come from the hand of God calculating and measuring; he came hungry.

From the beginning, then, Scripture affirms the reality and goodness of human hunger. Sin, of course, perverts our hunger, so that we seek to taste forbidden fruit rather than grasp the fruit of the tree of life, but sin does not change the fundamental realities of human desire. Our hearts follow where our treasure is; if what we value above all is in heaven, we will desire the Christ who is above, but if what we find most desirable are earthly things, our hearts will be focused on things below. Our lives are directed by our hungers, and we find rest only when we hunger for the One who opens His hand to satisfy the desire of every living thing more than we hunger for the things in His hand.

Yet, God has put us together in such a way that our hunger for the gift of food is designed to lead us to the Giver. Adam in Paradise was not told to stand aloof from food so that he could spend his time contemplating God in Himself. Adam was offered a world to eat and was expected to enjoy God in enjoying that bounty. Adam's sin was not eating; he sinned because he ate forbidden fruit, ate disobediently, ate without acknowledging God or giving thanks, ate as if food itself would lead him into a life of wisdom. Adam sinned because he was swayed by the tempter's claim that God was selfishly refusing to share the fruits of *this* tree with Adam. Adam's sin was all bound up with his suspicion that Yahweh's table was in the end no different from Marduk's.

When our hearts are renewed by the Spirit, desire is not eliminated but rightly directed, so that our desire for fellowship leads to the eternal communion of the Trinity, our hopes for honor to the glory of God, our search for knowledge to the One who is His Wisdom, our hunger for food to the bread from heaven.

This does not mean, however, that we are to purge our "material" hungers so that we may ascend to pure "spiritual" desires, or that our "secular" wants are to be "transcended" into "sacred" ones. As the Russian Orthodox theologian Alexander Schmemann wrote, with brilliant insight, "Nowhere in the Bible do we find the dichotomies which for us are the self-evident framework of all approaches to religion." Rather, "the food that man eats, the world of which he must partake in order to live, is given to him by God, and it is given as *communion with God*. . . . All that exists is God's gift to man, and it all exists to make God known to man, to make man's life communion with God. It is divine love made food, made life for man."

As a gift of food, the Lord's Supper discloses the inner meaning of all life and especially of all human life. Here the Lord shows that He alone is the Father of lights from whom proceeds all good and perfect gifts. Here He invites us to receive life from the Incarnate Word that has proceeded from Him. Here He confirms that all our hungers are satisfied in Him. Here, above all, relishing bread and wine *is* relishing the Gift that is the Giving God.

2

Feasting in Faith

And Melchizedek king of Salem brought out bread
and wine (Genesis 14:18).

The Reformers disagreed about the Lord's Supper more
than they disagreed about anything, but on one point there
was absolute unanimity: faith was considered an essential
element in the Supper. Exactly what role faith played was
debated among the Reformers, but none doubted it was
essential. Though the Reformation emphasis on faith was
a proper corrective to the superstitious tendencies of the
medieval Mass, the Reformers' view of faith tended to be
narrowly individualistic. Faith was required, according to
Calvin, if the individual believer was to commune with Christ
in the Supper. In Scripture, however, the connection between faith and the feast is set in a much more expansive
horizon. Faith is not only trusting God to save *me*, but
trusting God to do what He has promised to do in the
world. And what God has promised to do in the world is all
bound up with bread and wine.

We can get a fuller picture of this by looking at some
of the stories of Abram. Abram was a famously mobile character. Called from Ur of the Chaldees to Canaan, then commanded to leave his father behind in Haran, he finally entered

the land that the Lord promised to show him (Genesis 12:4). No sooner had he arrived, however, than he was on the move again. From a camp near Shechem, he traveled south to a location between Bethel and Ai, further south into the Negev, and then out of the land altogether. After a sojourn in Egypt, he returned, moving north and stopping at all his old haunts along the way (13:1, 3), until he finally settled for a time by the terebinths of Mamre near Hebron (13:18). Genesis 12 is a veritable travelogue, and chapter 13 retells the travelogue in reverse—all of which confirms the judgment of the writer to the Hebrews, who said that Abram lived by faith "as an alien in the land, as in a foreign land" (Hebrews 11:9).

Ceaseless wandering is bad, but Abram also faced other trials, trials that cast doubt on the truth of God's trustworthiness. Famine drove Abram into Egypt, as it later would also drive his descendants into Egypt. In the end, his sojourn in Egypt turned out well enough. When Pharaoh took Sarai into his house, Yahweh struck Pharaoh with plagues. Unable to cope, the Egyptian king sent Abram packing, but not before giving him "sheep and oxen and donkeys and male and female servants and female donkeys and camels" (12:16). So Abram plundered Egypt and returned to the land "very rich in livestock, in silver and in gold" (Genesis 13:2; cf. Exodus 12:35–36).

By the time he returned to the land, the famine was over, but almost immediately Abram found himself embroiled in a conflict with his nephew, Lot, because the land was still not able to sustain the flocks and herds of both men. Abram's "exodus," like the later exodus of Israel, was followed by family squabbles, and just as the Israelites strove with Moses in the wilderness because they lacked food and drink, so also the strife between the men of Abram and Lot arose because of a dearth of food. Abram wisely sought a peaceful separation before things got out of hand, but, adding insult to injury, Lot chose the better portion, the land toward the circle of the Jordan, which was "well watered everywhere . . . like the garden of the Lord" (13:10).

To put it mildly, the land had hardly lived up to its reputation. The Lord had brought Abram out of Haran with promises of blessing and possession, and throughout the Old Testament the land was the source of Israel's abundance, the land "flowing with milk and honey." But the land Abram found was famine-ridden and insufficiently productive to support two wealthy sheiks. How could it possibly feed a "great nation," like the one of which Abram was to be father? Abram was so cut off from the most fertile regions that he might as well have been sojourning in a desert.

Suddenly, things changed quite dramatically. Lot's decision to live in "Eden" was a foolish one, for Sodom proved to be a very fallen Eden. Lot ended up in the middle of a revolt against the territorial overlord, Chedorlaomer, king of Elam, and the twin cities of Sodom and Gomorrah were crushed in the ensuing war. Chedorlaomer took "all the goods of Sodom and Gomorrah and all their food supply," as well as Lot himself (14:11–12). When Abram received word of Lot's capture, he acted more like a conqueror than a sojourner. To our surprise, we learn that he had "trained men," three hundred and eighteen of them, whom he led north in pursuit. Being a competent military strategist, Abram divided his forces and launched a surprise attack (14:14–15), and Abram recovered Lot and his goods, along with the riches of Sodom, breaking forever Chedorlaomer's stranglehold on the land. Abram the alien became Abram the liberator.

On his way back from battle, Abram was met by the mysterious figure of Melchizedek, who came out with a gift of bread and wine, and, significantly, this is the first time we see Abram eating and drinking in the land. Purged by Abram's conquest, the land of famine and dearth became a land of plenty, full of wheat and wine. It is no accident that Melchizedek offered this meal to Abram in the "King's Valley" (14:17), for Abram's feast was a celebration of his victory, as he took his place as master of the land. Remembering this story as they camped on the plains of Moab waiting to cross the Jordan, the Israelites of a later generation took hope that the land would prove as rich as Yahweh had promised. They were assured that they, like their father Abram, would be exalted like stars in the firmament and that the famine that had driven Jacob from Canaan would be turned to feasting.

Like Lot, we were citizens of a fallen city and captives of a foreign power, but Jesus, the Seed of Abram, rescued us from the one who enslaved us, turned the desert land into Eden, and enthroned us as princes and princesses to feast in the Valley of Kings. He has won the definitive victory in His cross and resurrection, and bread and wine serve as His victory stele.

Celebrating a victory feast, however, seems more than a little premature. Within hours of the Last Supper, Jesus Himself was betrayed by one of His own disciples, arrested, slanderously accused, unjustly tried, tortured, and sentenced to crucifixion. Today, the world still seems more a wasteland than a garden, as we daily struggle to root up apparently intractable sins from our own hearts and contend with the evils from outside, within the church and in the world. Perhaps modern churches avoid celebrating the Supper for precisely this reason, because we have no confidence that the land is ours.

But a victory feast was no less premature for Abram, for his descendants would not conquer the land for several centuries. Yet Abram believed the God who brings life from the dead and ate a conqueror's meal in a land that was not yet his. All Christians know the Pauline dictim that "it is those who are of faith who are sons of Abraham" (Galatians 3:7). We must also embrace the truth that sons of Abraham not only live by faith, but feast in faith as well.

3
Memorial of the Lamb

Now this day will be a memorial to you, and you
shall celebrate it as a feast to Yahweh; throughout
your generations you are to celebrate it as an eternal ordinance (Exodus 12:14).

"Memory" in common speech normally refers to an inter-
nal mental process, but communities also "remember" things
together. These "social memories" help bind together the
members of a group, reinforcing their sense of a shared
past and present, and pointing them toward a shared future. Past events are not only "remembered" mentally but
are "re-enacted" in holidays and celebrations so that people
who were not alive at the time of the remembered events
get a feeling of belonging. Fireworks on the Fourth of July
recall our war for independence and leave us with the sense
of being part of a grand experiment in human liberty. Eating and drinking in the church is a ritual memory of the
death of Christ and reminds us of the story of which we
are a new chapter.

Important as this perspective is to understanding how
the Supper molds the church as a unified people, these social dynamics cannot give a complete picture of the "com-
memorative" aspect of the sacrament. The Supper is not

merely a human rite, and humans are not the only active participants. At the Lord's table, children eat food provided by our heavenly Father, and the bride communes with her Husband through the power of the Spirit. Insofar as it is a memorial, the Supper involves both the church and the Triune God in whom we live and move.

But how is the Supper a "memorial" that involves both God and His church? Consideration of the Passover meal provides some insight. It virtually goes without saying that Jesus died to fulfill Passover. John the Baptist called Jesus the Passover lamb (John 1:29); John's gospel records that this Lamb was being slaughtered at the same time that the Jews were busy preparing their Passover lambs (John 19:14; cf. Exodus 12:3–6); and, as if these hints were not sufficient, Paul tells us plainly that "Christ our Passover is sacrificed for us" (1 Corinthians 5:7). By shedding His blood on the cross, Jesus turned away the angel of death and rescued us from the wrath of God. Merely shedding blood, however, was not enough to turn away the final plague. If the Passover was going to "work," blood had to be displayed on the door frame of the house, and this principle is reflected everywhere in the sacrificial system as well. True, "without the shedding of blood there is no forgiveness"; but it is equally true that "without the display of blood there is no redemption" (e.g., Leviticus 1:5; 3:2; 4:5–7; etc.).

When we try to explain how the death of Jesus fulfills Passover in this sense, we are left with something of a puzzle. According to the book of Hebrews, Jesus displayed His blood in the heavenly tabernacle (Hebrews 9:11–28), but this fulfilled the ritual of the Day of Atonement, not the ritual of Passover. We might say that the cross itself, or perhaps the earth, served as "lintel and doorposts" at this

Passover, but that seems to imply that salvation is universal, that everyone on earth is within the blood-marked house
of Israel. Or, we might give up and conclude that the Passover is fulfilled in general but not in its specific ritual details.

When we recall that the Passover was not only a type
of Christ's death but also of the Lord's Supper, we can
approach a better answer to these questions. Jesus instituted the Supper at a meal associated with Passover (Luke
22:1, 14–15), and this was the climax to Jesus' practice
of celebrating alternative Passovers with His followers (cf.
John 6:1–14). Paul confirmed this link when he followed
the declaration that Christ is our Passover with the exhortation to "keep the feast . . . with the unleavened bread of
sincerity and truth" (1 Corinthians 5:8).

The Supper of the church is a new Passover not only
because we consume the flesh and blood of the Lamb of
God but also because it, like the Passover, is a "memorial"
meal. To many, this suggests that the annual Passover was
designed to remind Israel of her great deliverance from Egypt,
and this was certainly one effect of the holiday (Exodus
12:24–27). In Scripture, however, a "memorial" is not
primarily designed to remind people of God's works, but
to remind God of His words. The first memorial mentioned in the Bible was the rainbow that God set in the sky
after the flood as a "sign of the covenant." God explained
how it would work: "When the bow is in the cloud, then I
will look upon it, to remember the everlasting covenant
between God and every living creature" (Genesis 9:16).
The bow served as a memorial to God, not to Noah and his
sons.

Similarly, in the sacrificial system, "memorials" were
directed toward God, not toward the worshipers.

A handful of the grain offering was burned on the altar, ascending to Yahweh in smoke, and this was called the "memorial portion" (Leviticus 2:2, 9, 16; cf. 5:12). A priest put the memorial on the altar so that it could be a "food offering of a soothing aroma to Yahweh" (Leviticus 2:2; my translation). In the New Testament, Cornelius's prayers and alms also went up before the Lord as a "memorial" (Acts 10:31).

In this same sense, the annual Passover meal was a memorial of the Exodus. Whenever Israel celebrated the Passover, she was conscious that she lived in a dangerous world, threatened in various ways by her own sin and by the powerful nations that surrounded her. As Israel kept this feast, she was re-enacting before Yahweh the meal of her deliverance, reminding Him of how He fulfilled His covenant in bringing her from Egypt, calling on Him to act again and again on her behalf, urging Him to remember His covenant. When Yahweh "remembered" His covenant with Israel, He would bare His arm to fight for her (cf. Exodus 3:6–9). Each Passover, in short, was a cry for a new exodus. Of course, it was not enough for Israel to call on God to fight for her. Since Israel had sinned, she also had to call on Yahweh for forgiveness. When she celebrated the feast of Passover at the tabernacle and temple, the blood displayed on the altar was a "memorial," calling on God to forgive her sins. As Yahweh drew near, He would "see the blood" and "pass over" her sins.

When Jesus instituted the Lord's Supper, He called it His "memorial" (Luke 22:19; 1 Corinthians 11:24–25), and this should be understood in the same sense as Old Testament "memorials." Our meal is not designed in the first place to remind *us* of what Jesus has done, though it does and by doing that it constantly renews our memory of the cross and the empty tomb. Essentially, though, the Supper is not a meal to help us remember; it is a memorial meal. Like the Passover, it is directed to the Father, "reminding" Him of the covenant sealed in the blood of His Son, calling on Him to draw near and act for us. The blood of Christ was shed once-for-all, but each time we break bread and drink wine before the Father, we display the tokens of Christ's sacrifice to "remind" the Father of that once-for-all act. Seeing the blood of the true Lamb, He renews His covenant and announces His forgiveness afresh. Seeing the blood of the Lamb, He passes over and carries out His judgments against Egypt.

4

Holy Things
for the Holy Ones

No stranger is to eat the holy; a sojourner with the
priest or a hired man shall not eat of the holy. But
if a priest buys a slave as property with his money,
that one may eat of it, and those who are born in
his house may eat of his bread (Leviticus 22:10–
11).

"Holy things for the holy ones." By these ancient words,
the saints of the early church were invited to receive the
Lord's body and blood at the Lord's table. The "holy elements" of bread and wine were being offered to the "holy
people." Though the phrase may seem to be little more than
an arcane bit of liturgical history, it is in fact among the
most radical statements in the history of man. Too radical,
it seems, for Christians to grasp fully, for by the sixth
century women had been forbidden to touch the Eucharistic bread, and in the tenth-century *Ordo Romanus VI*, the
privilege of touching the elements was reserved to bishops,
priests, and deacons. Consecrated bread and wine had come
to be *too* holy for anyone but a consecrated cleric to approach.

  The radical character of this liturgical pronouncement

eludes us, however, unless we understand something about the order of holiness that structured Old Testament Israel. From the time that the tabernacle was constructed at Mount Sinai, Israel was organized according to what one scholar has called a system of "graded holiness," a religious zoning map of the world. Every place and everything in the world fit somewhere on the map. At the center of the world was the tabernacle, the holiest place within the holy camp, the tent where Yahweh was enthroned in glory. This tent was divided into three zones, which had different degrees of holiness. The inner sanctum of the tabernacle, called the Most Holy Place, was the holiest of all; the first room, called the Holy Place, was of a lesser degree of holiness; and the courtyard surrounding the tent, even less. When Israel entered the land and set up a permanent sanctuary, that became the center of Israel's holiness system, and the land was mapped out from this central point—and not only the land, but the whole world. Go north toward the Sea of Galilee and space gets less holy; move toward Yahweh's glory in the tabernacle and you begin to tread on holy ground.

Among other things, the word "holy" means "unapproachable," and Israel's holiness map was partly intended to keep most people away from the center, to protect sinners from being in the presence of a holy God. Similar grades of holiness were thus applied to persons. Corresponding to the Most Holy Place was the "most holy man," the High Priest, who alone was permitted to enter the inner sanctuary on the Day of Atonement (Leviticus 16:2). Other priests entered the outer room to perform a variety of tasks, and priests were also allowed to approach the bronze altar in the tabernacle courtyard to offer sacrifices on it. Though every Israelite was a priest (Exodus 19:6), only the Aaronic priests were allowed to serve at the altar. Corresponding to the degrees of holy space (Most Holy Place, Holy Place, and Courtyard), then, was a hierarchy of holy people (High Priest, priests, and lay Israelites).

Food was one of the marks of holiness for persons, for it too was categorized by the system of graded holiness. Flesh from a "sin offering," for example, was classified as "most holy" and could be eaten only by the priests and only in a holy place (Leviticus 6:26, 29). Portions from other sacrifices, classified as "holy," could be eaten by the members of a priest's household (Leviticus 22:10–16). Meat from the peace offering could be eaten by an Israelite worshiper (Leviticus 7:11–18), because the flesh of the peace offering did not have any "holy" status at all. Rules about food thus followed the boundary lines of the holiness system, and keeping the unholy from receiving holy food was an important part of guarding the holiness of Israel. Under the Old Covenant, "holy things to holy people" meant "holy food for the priests."

Israel was not the only ancient people organized according to such principles. Many ancient societies mapped out the world in ways similar to Israel, with a temple at the *axis mundi* and the rest of the world radiating out from there. Though we think of the ancient Greeks as arch-rationalists, for example, there is plenty of evidence that they were as haunted by fears of uncleanness and violations of holy space as any Jew. Greek cities were dotted with sacred pillars, images, and temples, all of which had to be guarded from pollution with the same vigilance as the tabernacle of Yahweh.

The Christian gospel is the announcement that this whole system has been undone by the cross and resurrection of Christ. In the cross, He has broken down "the barrier of the dividing wall" that separated Jews and Gentiles, and in doing so, He has torn the veil that separated priests and people. Having obliterated this wall on the cross, Jesus forms "one new man" from the two races of the old world so that Gentiles who believe are now "fellow citizens with the holy ones." Instead of a wall, Jesus is building a temple, using Jews and Gentiles as his building blocks (Ephesians 2:11–22), and in this temple, all believers in Jesus shine like the lamps of a lampstand. Jesus, in short, rezoned the world from the cross; from the cross, Jesus began to form a new sort of people and a new sort of world.

As in the Old Testament, the religious mapping described in the New Testament is manifested in rules about food. While the Old Covenant restricted access to holy food, the New is an open invitation to the feast. In place of the many meals with various rules for access, there is now only one holy meal, and this meal is now offered to all who are holy ones in the Holy One. Each time we observe the Supper as Jesus directed, we are celebrating the gospel of the torn veil and the broken wall. But we are doing more than celebrating it. By including all the holy ones at the holy feast, we are enacting the New Covenant, becoming the one body that we are, the one body where there is neither Jew nor Greek, slave nor free, male nor female. Each time we celebrate this meal, we are furthering Christ's work of rezoning the world.

"Holy things for the holy ones," indeed.

5

Jealousy Test

Then [the priest] shall make the woman drink the water of bitterness that brings a curse, so that the water which brings a curse will go into her and cause bitterness (Numbers 5:24).

It is one of the most famous scenes of medieval history: Emperor Henry IV standing barefoot in the snow outside the castle gates of Canossa, doing penance and waiting for absolution from the imperious Pope, Gregory VII. Eventually, Henry's humiliation paid off, and his excommunication was lifted. The aftermath of this dramatic encounter is not, however, nearly so well known. Since charges were still outstanding against Gregory himself, as Henry Charles Lea tells it in his engrossing little book, *The Ordeal*, the Pope said that he could easily refute them by abundant witnesses:

> but lest I should seem to rely rather on human than on divine testimony, and that I may remove from the minds of all, by immediate satisfaction, every scruple, behold this body of our Lord which I am about to take. Let it be to me this day a test of my innocence, and may the Omnipotent God this day by his judgment absolve me of the accusations if I

am innocent, or let me perish in sudden death if guilty.

Gregory swallowed the wafer without incident, then turned to offer it to Henry, accompanied by the same oath. The Emperor declined, perhaps remembering an incident in the previous year when William, the Bishop of Utrecht, excommunicated Gregory, "but when," Lea writes, "at the conclusion of the impious ceremony, [William] audaciously took the Host, it turned to fire within him, and, shrieking, 'I burn! I burn!' he fell down and miserably died."

Medieval chronicles are rich with legends of this sort, which are to us more bemusing than instructive. However much perverted by superstition, the medieval church had grasped an important biblical insight: God tests His people with food. In the wilderness, Moses declared to Israel that the Lord "humbled you and let you be hungry, and fed you with manna which you did not know, nor did your fathers know, that He might make you understand that man does not live by bread alone, but man lives by everything that proceeds out of the mouth of the Lord" (Deuteronomy 8:3). Earlier, God had put Adam to a food test, which, like Israel, he miserably failed. Testing loyalty through food is no arbitrary choice on God's part. A food test sharply poses the question: will we seek blessing from the Word that comes from the mouth of God, or will we seek it from the food that perishes? Food is a test of faith because food is life.

A food test of a different sort is found in the law in Numbers 5, a law known as a "jealousy test." Here, a woman is tested not by hunger but by drinking a sacred mixture. An Israelite man who suspected that his wife had been unfaithful to him was required to take her to the priest, along with one-tenth of an ephah of barley meal. The priest would put a handful of dust from the tabernacle floor into an earthenware vessel full of holy water. Standing with loosed hair and with the grain offering in her hand, the woman would take a "self-maledictory" oath, an oath of "self-cursing." Then the priest would write the curses on a scroll and wash the scroll off in the holy water. While the priest offered a memorial portion of the grain to the Lord, the woman would drink the water. If she had committed adultery, the holy water would "go into her stomach and make her abdomen swell and her thigh waste away" (5:22). Holy water bearing a curse came into contact with the polluted woman, and her pollution became visible.

Specifically, the charge against the woman in Numbers 5 is not adultery but harlotry. The word "to go astray" in Numbers 5:12 is used elsewhere only in connection with prostitution (see Proverbs 4:15; 7:25). This law is thus linked with the vivid prophetic passages that use the imagery of whoredom to describe the unfaithfulness of Israel (see Jeremiah 2:20–25; Ezekiel 16; 23; Micah 1:7). Numbers 5 not only reveals a legal procedure but also tells us something about the way that the Lord tests and exposes His unfaithful bride. We see a glimpse of this in the golden calf incident at Sinai. When Moses discovered that Israel was going after the gods of Egypt, he was provoked to outraged jealousy; he destroyed the calf, ground it to powder, scattered the powder over the waters, and forced Israel to drink the water (Exodus 32:20). Israel had provoked the Lord to jealousy by celebrating a feast before the golden calf, and now her harlotry was being exposed by a jealousy rite. Israelites who had participated in idolatry were mercilessly slaughtered.

Like Israel, Jesus was put to a food test in the wilderness (Matthew 4:1–11). As the true Israel and the

Last Adam, He overcame the temptation, relying on His heavenly Father rather than succumbing to Satan's temptation to grasp forbidden fruit. Because He fasted, we are admitted to the feast.

But the feast that we enjoy is still a jealousy rite. Moses sprinkled the powdered gold from the calf into the water flowing from the rock (see Exodus 17:6), the water that had turned the Sinai wilderness into a well-watered garden. The same water that was life to Israel became death to the many who went astray. According to Paul, this water from the rock was a type of the drink we receive in the Lord's Supper: "All ate the same spiritual food; and all drank the same spiritual drink, for they were drinking from a spiritual rock which followed them; and the rock was Christ" (1 Corinthians 10:3–4). His description of the sins of Israel in the wilderness included a specific reference to the golden calf incident: "Do not be idolaters, as some of them were; as it is written, 'The people sat down to eat and drink, and stood up to play'" (1 Corinthians 10:7; see Exodus 32:6). A few short verses later, Paul warned the Corinthians to "flee from idolatry," since it would "provoke the Lord to jealousy" (1 Corinthians 10:14, 22). When we act as Israel did, joining ourselves with the table of demons, we commit harlotry and the Lord, our Husband, is provoked to jealous and righteous wrath. Our food and drink at the Lord's table will "test us, to see what is on our hearts."

And we may fail the test. Perhaps the most famous New Testament passage concerning the Lord's Supper is 1 Corinthians 11:23–32, where Paul sternly warned the Corinthians not to partake of the Supper unworthily. Misuse of this passage has robbed many Christians of the joy of the Lord's Supper, but we should not react to misuse by ignoring the passage altogether. Some Corinthians, Paul reminded them, were sick and some were even dead because they did not judge the body rightly, because they had committed the same sins that Israel committed, because they had joined themselves to demons. Some, Paul might have said, had swollen stomachs and wasted legs. Communion bread is unlikely to turn to fire in our stomachs, but that does not make this event any less solemn. At this table, the Lord offers us the life-giving water from the stricken Rock, but by our sin we can make this gift into a "water of bitterness that brings a curse."

Jealousy is zeal to protect one's possessions. To say that God is jealous means not only that He indignantly refuses to share His bride, but that He protects and cares for her with a love that is breathtaking for its passionate intensity. When He spreads a table for His bride, He is not only subjecting her to a test of faithfulness, but displaying that fierce love. As we come in humble faith, the Supper is our assurance that the Lord is our jealous Husband, who will allow nothing to seize His bride from Him. It assures us that nothing—life or death, principalities or powers, things present or things to come—will ever separate us from His love in Christ Jesus.

6

Proclaiming the
Priest's Death

After the death of the high priest the manslayer
shall return to the land of his possession (Numbers 35:28).

From the time of Noah, it has been a basic principle of
biblical justice that "whoever sheds man's blood, by man
shall his blood be shed," and this principle is rooted in the
nature of man as "the image of God" (Genesis 9:6). Under the Mosaic system, not only murder but other crimes
were punished by death, including adultery and sodomy,
religious offenses such as transgressing holy ground, blas-
phemy, and certain forms of Sabbath breaking. It is even
arguable that the death penalty was at the heart of the entire Old Testament system. Because Israel was the holy
possession of God, the nation among whom the Lord dwelt,
anything that polluted Yahweh or His house had to be cut
off from Israel. With God living in her midst, Israel had to
be extra careful to purge sin. No wonder Paul called the
Law a "ministry of death" and a "ministry of condemnation" (2 Corinthians 3:7–11).

Though the Mosaic system of justice is stern by modern standards, a number of provisions moderated its

effects. Among these was the institution of the "city of refuge." When Israel entered the land, they set apart six cities that would serve this purpose, three in the Transjordan and three in Canaan proper (Numbers 35:14–15). When someone was killed, a near relative served as an "avenger of blood." As an agent of the land, his duty was to carry out capital punishment and thereby purge the land of the guilt of innocent blood. But the Bible makes a firm distinction between premeditated murder and an accidental killing. An Israelite guilty of manslaughter could flee to the nearest city of refuge to stand trial. If the city officials determined that he was innocent of murder, he was allowed to live in the city of refuge, protected from the avenger of blood so long as he remained within the city. When the High Priest died, the manslayer was allowed to leave the city of refuge and return to his land (Numbers 35:28). The death of the High Priest cleansed the land of innocent blood, allowing the fugitive to return to his inheritance and escape the penalty of death.

This law casts intriguing light on Israel's sojourn in the wilderness. For forty years after their refusal to enter the land, Israel was not permitted to cross the Jordan to enter Canaan. Immediately after the death of Aaron, however, Israel fought with the king of Arad and won a great victory (Numbers 20:22–21:3). Their trials and temptations were far from over, for immediately after this triumph they grumbled against the Lord and were ravaged by serpents (Numbers 21:4–9). But the conquest of Canaan had begun—after the death of the High Priest. The wilderness was a kind of "city of refuge," where Israel was confined until the death of Aaron. Once the High Priest died, she began to enter into her inheritance.

The death of a leader is normally a moment of crisis, a

dangerous moment of interruption and uncertainty. When Moses died, Yahweh took special pains to demonstrate to Israel that Joshua was a worthy successor. When Joshua died, Israel lapsed into complacency and left much of the land unconquered. After each judge died, Israel quickly turned again to idols, and when Saul died, the Philistines took the cities from Israel (1 Samuel 31:7). But the death of a High Priest is contrary to all normal expectation. Even the death of Eli, the High Priest who made himself fat with stolen sacrificial flesh and honored his sons above Yahweh, marked a turning point in Israel's history. Though the Philistines captured the ark on the day of Eli's death, it soon returned with spoils (1 Samuel 4–6), and at the next battle with Philistia, the Israelites retook the cities the Philistines had captured (1 Samuel 7:14). No matter that Eli was an ineffectual priest: at the death of the High Priest, God's favor began to rest on Israel.

At the Lord's table, Paul said, we proclaim a death (1 Corinthians 11:26), but that is only good news if the death we proclaim is the death of a High Priest. And it is: at this meal, we proclaim the death of the Priest after the order of Melchizedek. By His death, the ministry of condemnation and death has given way to the ministry of righteousness and life. By His death, the death sentence that was over us is torn up and thrown away (Colossians 2:14). By His death, He has cleansed the land and released us from our wilderness refuge to enter into our inheritance. All this, and more, we proclaim when we eat this bread and drink this cup.

7

Land of Milk and Honey

And the manna ceased on the day after they had
eaten some of the produce of the land, so that the
sons of Israel no longer had manna, but they ate
some of the yield of the land of Canaan during that
year (Joshua 5:12).

Entering the land meant many things to ancient Israel. Land
provided a national home, where Israel's hosts could spread
out, settle, and find Sabbath rest. Establishment in the land
gave Israel a political base on which to build herself into a
significant regional power. Once in the land, Israel could
establish God's house in a permanent location, where she
could bring burnt offerings and peace offerings and celebrate feasts in the presence of the Lord. By bringing Israel to the land, God fulfilled promises made to Abraham,
Isaac, and Jacob and proved Himself to be Yahweh, the God
who keeps covenant.

Throughout the Pentateuch, though, the promise of
land is preeminently a promise of food. When Yahweh appeared to Moses at the burning bush, He promised to deliver Israel from Egypt and bring them north into a "good
and spacious land, to a land flowing with milk and honey"
(Exodus 3:8). As Israel celebrated the first Passover and

prepared to leave Egypt, Moses commanded them to observe the feast when they entered the "land flowing with milk and honey" (Exodus 13:5). When Israel rebelled at Kadesh, the ten spies acknowledged that the land was as rich and fruitful as Yahweh had promised, though they doubted they could conquer it (Numbers 13:27–28). Korah charged that Moses had not kept His promise: "You have not brought us to a land flowing with milk and honey." To Korah, Egypt was such a land, but Moses had enticed Israel from the garden of Egypt "to have us die in the wilderness" (Numbers 16:13–14). But the truth was otherwise, as Moses emphasized:

> Yahweh your God is bringing you into a good land, a land of brooks of water, of fountains and springs, flowing forth in valleys and hills; a land of wheat and barley, of vines and fig trees and pomegranates, a land of olive oil and honey; a land where you shall eat food without scarcity, in which you shall not lack anything . . . . When you have eaten and are satisfied, you shall bless the Lord your God for the good land which He has given you. (Deuteronomy 8:7–10)

Centuries before, Lot saw that the land toward Sodom was like the garden of God, well-watered throughout (Genesis 13:10). The land promised to Israel was richer still, a land fed by streams of milk whose rocks dripped honey. From the first, land meant food. From the moment dry land appeared on the third day of creation, it began to produce fruit and grain, food to strengthen and gladden man. When Adam was set in the garden, he was offered every tree producing fruit as food, excepting only the tree of knowledge. Entering the land as the new Adamic people, Israel likewise was offered an abundance of food.

Fittingly, one of Israel's first acts upon entering the land was to celebrate a feast. Joshua, a new Moses, led Israel through the waters of the Jordan, and when they had crossed, he circumcised them in preparation for Passover (Joshua 5:4–10). Once they had "rolled away" the reproach of Egypt, Israel was ready to celebrate the feast memorializing their deliverance from Egypt.

After the first Passover, Israel entered the wilderness where the Lord provided manna from heaven and water from the rock; after the first Passover in the land, manna ceased, and in its place, Israel "ate some of the produce of the land, unleavened cakes and parched grain" (Joshua 5:11). Though Israel's bread would henceforward come from the earth, instead of from the sky, fundamentally nothing had changed. Food from the land was as dependent upon the Lord's generosity, and even as miraculous, as manna in the wilderness. As Moses emphasized, Israel was entering a land full of "great and splendid cities which you did not build . . . vineyards and olive trees which you did not plant" (Deuteronomy 6:10–11). Unlike Egypt, which depended on the earth-water of the Nile for its fertility, Canaan "drinks water from the rain of heaven" (Deuteronomy 11:10–11). Manna ceased on the day after this first Passover in Canaan, but the milk and honey of the land was also food from heaven.

Altogether an audacious move, this feast of Joshua not only left Israel utterly vulnerable to Canaanite attack (see Genesis 34 to find out what could happen to recently circumcised men!), but, even more, Israel moved across the river and immediately began using the land as if it all belonged to her. Before the first battle was fought, before one city had fallen under the ban, before a single home had been built or a single garden planted, the land had already become a place for feasting. Before she had won rest from her enemies, Israel was acting as if she already had plenty of time to laze around eating and drinking. When she finally got down to the business of conquest, Israel was acting as if the conquest were over; Israel girded on armor as one who removes armor. Audacious, to be sure, but this is the audacity of faith.

Jesus is, of course, the true manna, the true bread from heaven, whose flesh and blood nourishes us to everlasting life (John 6:32–59). And He is also our true land. Adam was formed from earth, and the earth, his "mother," suckled him. We are formed from the new, living "ground" of Jesus, and from Him we receive our bread. Having passed through the waters of Jordan in baptism, we begin to enjoy the produce of our land, the bread and wine that is the body and blood of Jesus. Planted into this land, we begin to share in the abundant life given by the Father.

Our meal is every bit as audacious as Joshua's. In the New Covenant, our inheritance encompasses all things. All is Christ's, and He is ours, and so all is ours (1 Corinthians 3:21–23). In and with Him, we are heirs of the nations, the uttermost parts of the earth. As the land was given to Israel, so the world has been given to us as our "food," gifts for abundant life. And, just as Israel feasted in the land before she conquered it, so we feast in the midst of our inheritance before we receive our inheritance in full. We do not yet see the Canaanites put under the ban, nor do we see the saints riding the high places of the earth. But what we do see is enough: we see a new Israel sitting at the table of a greater Joshua, feasting on the firstfruits of our inheritance. And in this we proclaim with audacious hope that in time the world will be ours.

8
Showbread and Sonship

> So the priest gave [David] consecrated bread; for
> there was no bread there but the bread of the Pres-
> ence which was removed from before the Lord, in
> order to put hot bread when it was taken away (1
> Samuel 21:6).

Conflict between fathers and sons is a central theme in a
fair portion of the world's literature. Even those who have
little sympathy for Freud have to be impressed with the
frequent appearance of the Oedipus theme in literature and
myth. In Shakespeare's play, Hamlet's life is stretched out
between the demands of his ghost-father and the obstacles
thrown up by his murderer-uncle-stepfather. One of the
earliest of English novels, *Robinson Crusoe*, is in part a retelling of the prodigal son story, and other early English
novels, such as those of Henry Fielding and Samuel
Richardson, follow the biblical parable even more closely.
Dostoevsky's masterpiece, *The Brothers Karamazov*, is concerned not only with the brothers of the title but with
their variously shaded relations with their sensualist father,
Fyodor, and in this Dostoevsky was ringing changes on a
theme already developed by his contemporary, Ivan Turgenev.
    Theologically, history as a whole can be seen as the

dramatic story of a father and his sons, as a dynamic between filial estrangement and adoption. Adam, God's son,
sinned against his Father and lost his inheritance, but in
Christ, the Son, mankind is received back into the family
of the Father. As Brian Gerrish has pointed out, Calvin's
theology is structured by this story, and this gives his entire theology a "eucharistic shape," since the sign of our
adoption is that God welcomes us back to His house and
His table.

A microcosm of this broad biblical story is found in I
Samuel, a book nearly overflowing with father-son conflicts. In this respect, as in many others, the early chapters
of I Samuel are a retelling of the story of Genesis. After
the fall of Babel (Genesis 11), God called Abram to be the
father of a new nation and the head of a new covenant. I
Samuel begins with a focus on the shrine at Shiloh, which
itself involved a tragic story of a father and his sons. After
the destruction of this sacred place, which had been the
center of Israel's worship from the time of the conquest
(Joshua 18:1), the Lord called Samuel to be a new Abram,
the father of a renewed Israel and the mediator of a renewed covenant.

Samuel was a new Abram, and Saul was another Isaac.
When Saul wandered into Samuel's hometown of Ramah
looking for his father's donkeys, Samuel "adopted" Saul
into his household and treated him as a son by setting him
at the head of the table and giving him an honorific portion of the sacrifice (I Samuel 9:22–24). After Saul was
found among the prophets, people asked, "Who is their
father?"(I Samuel 10:11–12). Samuel, of course, was the
father of the prophets, and by being inducted into their
band, Saul became a member of Samuel's household. Saul,
first introduced dutifully caring for his father's donkeys,

was now to follow the instructions of his "father" Samuel.

Following the story of Samuel and his "son," we have the story of Saul and his sons, and, like the story of Isaac, this is largely a story about the sins of the father. In spite of the fact that the Lord had revealed that the elder would serve the younger, Isaac persistently favored Esau—significantly enough, because Esau provided him with tasty food. Isaac was a man ruled by his belly, a man going blind who could not distinguish between Jacob and Esau, a man whose eyes had been closed so that he could not discern good and evil.

Saul was not physically blind, but he was as spiritually blind as Isaac, and as with Isaac, Saul's lack of discernment was evident especially in his assessment of his sons—his biological son, Jonathan, and his son-in-law, David. Saul wanted to put Jonathan to death because he had eaten some honey during a battle, violating the fast that Saul had foolishly imposed on his army (1 Samuel 14). For Saul, it did not matter that Jonathan was the hero of the battle with the Philistines; he ate forbidden food and must die. Saul's treatment of Jonathan foreshadows his later treatment of David, another Israelite war hero. Saul became enraged at David's success, tried to kill him several times, and accused him of conspiracy against the throne. Saul could not recognize a faithful son when he saw one, but drove both of these sons from his house and from his table.

In another respect, the story of Saul and David recapitulates the story of Israel in Egypt. After initially welcoming Israel into the land and giving them the land of Goshen for their possession, Egypt eventually turned hostile. Yahweh delivered Israel with great plagues and wonders, and Israel had to flee from Pharaoh's house by night. Having escaped through the Red Sea, Israel entered the

wilderness, where God provided miraculous bread and water throughout forty years of wandering. And so it is with
David. Escaping from Saul's house was an "exodus" from a
king who was acting like Pharaoh. Driven from Saul, David
went into the wilderness and wandered for years before finally entering the land to conquer it.

Though David was driven from his father's house and
forced into exile, he was in fact the true Israel, the true
"son of God," and his growing band of followers was the
core of a new nation. Throughout David's wilderness years,
the Lord showed His faithfulness to His anointed, providing bread in the wilderness. When David stopped at the
priestly city of Nob, south of Saul's capital city of Gibeah,
the priests provided David with showbread from the tabernacle. Set out fresh each Sabbath on the golden table in
the light of the golden lampstand, the showbread was the
Sabbath food of the priests (Leviticus 24:5–9). By law,
eating showbread was one of the privileges of being a priest,
a member of God's household, but David was also permitted to eat it. As bread fell from heaven for Israel, bread
from the "firmament" of the tabernacle was given to David
and his band. In both cases, bread was a sign of God's favor
to His "son."

Jesus cited this incident in a debate with the Pharisees
about Sabbath-keeping (Matthew 12:1–8). David evidently
arrived in Nob on a Sabbath day, for old showbread was
available only on the Sabbath. In reminding the Pharisees
of this incident, however, Jesus was not only concerned
with the issue of Sabbath-keeping. In addition, He was over-
turning the Pharisees' view of their place in Israel. The
Pharisees considered themselves the true sons of God, who
followed their Father's example by rigorously keeping Sabbath
laws. Jesus saw them in a different light: Jesus was putting

the Pharisees in the place of Saul, the enemy of God, who attacked David and never learned the lesson that God "desires compassion and not sacrifice" (Matthew 12:7; see I Samuel 15:22–23). By referring to this incident, Jesus not only raised the question of Sabbath-keeping but posed the issue of sonship: who are the true sons, the Pharisees who criticize the disciples or the disciples of the "Son of Man"? Who is the true Israel, David or Saul?

Our world, like Jesus', is full of Sauls, apostates hostile to the Lord's Christ and to His faithful people. Still today, many must hate father and mother in order to cling to Christ, and many are disowned and persecuted by their own families for this choice. But still today, the true Israel receives bread from heaven, a sign that we are sons of God and brothers of a greater David. Every time we sit at this table and eat the true showbread, the true "bread of the presence," the Lord is declaring to us that we are His children, and we are declaring to the world that He is our Father. Estranged though David was from his father the king, he was always welcome at the table of his Father the King. Estranged though we may be from our earthly father's house, here we find a true family table.

9

Continual Feasting

> Judah and Israel were as numerous as the sand that
> is on the seashore in abundance; they were eating
> and drinking and rejoicing (1 Kings 4:20).

Solomon's reign was the culmination of Israel's previous
history. During his reign, the promise to Abraham that
Israel would be like sand on the seashore was fulfilled (1
Kings 4:20). During his reign, Israel's borders expanded
so that Solomon ruled over all the kingdoms from the River
to the land of the Philistines and to the border of Egypt"
(1 Kings 4:21), boundaries that map out the land promised to Abraham (Genesis 15:18). As Yahweh had promised, Abraham's seed became a blessing to the nations, for
"men came from all peoples to hear the wisdom of Solomon"
(1 Kings 4:34). Solomon's temple was the climax of the
Exodus from Egypt; this is indicated by the fact that the
building of the temple is dated as the "four hundred and
eightieth year after the sons of Israel came out of the land
of Egypt" (1 Kings 6:1). During his reign, the conquest
of the land came to final completion, for David had subdued Israel's enemies on every side, so that Israel could dwell
in safety in the land, "every man under his vine and fig tree"
(1 Kings 4:25). Solomon's reign was even the climax of

the previous history of man. Solomon was exalted to rule and thereby fulfilled the Adamic commission to rule the earth in wisdom.

In the description of the prosperity of Israel under Solomon in 1 Kings 4, many of these earlier promises are mentioned or alluded to. At the center of the description are two related emphases: the abundance of food that Solomon and Israel enjoyed and their safety from enemies round about. This focus is brought out by the structure of the passage. 1 Kings 4:20–34 is framed by references to the "sand that is on the seashore" and is arranged chiastically:

> Judah and Israel numerous as sand, v. 20a
>   food, vv. 20b–23
>   Solomon's dominion, v. 24a
>   Peace in Israel, vv. 24b–25
>   Solomon's army, v. 26
>   food, vv. 27–28
> Solomon's wisdom like sand, vv. 29–34

Israel as a whole was "eating and drinking and rejoicing," as if the reign of Solomon were one continuous party, and Solomon himself had an astonishingly rich daily provision: "Thirty kors of fine flour and sixty kors of meal, ten fat oxen, twenty pasture-fed oxen, a hundred sheep besides deer, gazelles, roebucks, and fattened fowl" (vv. 23–24). This list of food reminds us of the lists of food in Leviticus that describe provisions for the sanctuary worship. In Leviticus, the lists highlight the abundant provision for Yahweh's table, His "bread," and 1 Kings shows us that Solomon shared in that abundance as Yahweh's anointed king and "son" (cf. 2 Samuel 7:14). He was the prince of the One who is enthroned above the firmament.

Solomon's table was supplied not only with sacrificial animals (oxen and sheep) but clean, nonsacrificial meats. Deer, gazelle, and roebuck were all wild animals that Israel was free to eat, even though these animals were not allowed on the altar (Deuteronomy 14:5). In the Old Testament, these animals symbolized God-fearing Gentiles, just as the sacrificial animals symbolized Israelites, and unclean animals—predators such as lions, for example—signified unbelievers. It is no accident, then, that the description of Solomon's table is followed by a reference to his dominion over "everything west of the River." Solomon incorporated "Gentile" land into Israel, and his table was, appropriately, laden with "Gentile" food. Solomon gobbled up Gentile territory into the kingdom of Israel.

Continuous feasting was thus a sign of the peace Israel enjoyed because her enemies had been subdued or converted (see 1 Kings 5:1–12; see 4:24a–25). This was a comparatively new thing in Israel's history. Throughout the period of the judges, the nations surrounding Israel were continually invading and enslaving her, and at times invaders plundered Israel, leaving her without food (see Judges 6:3–5). Due to these invasions, the land of plenty was often in want. David, however, had now subdued all these enemies, so that Israel was plundered no more, and under David's son, she could enjoy her produce without fear. On the heels of David's victories, Solomon could proclaim the feast and invite the Queen of the South to share his table (1 Kings 10). Solomon's evangelism centers on the table: gentiles are invited to partake of the life of the kingdom, offered in the feast of the kingdom.

Near the beginning of Luke's gospel are several songs that express the hope that a new David, a new lion of Judah, will come to trample Israel's enemies, and that a new

Solomon will come to reign over a land enjoying peace and safety. The Lord, Mary sings, "has done mighty deeds with His arm; He has scattered those who were proud in the thoughts of their heart"(Luke 1:51). And Zecharias rejoices that the covenant has been fulfilled, the covenant that promised "that we, being delivered from the hand of our enemies, might serve Him without fear, in holiness and righteousness before Him all our days" (1:74–75). Jesus is the fulfillment of those hopes. Because there is a King enthroned above the firmament, a Son of David who rules from sea to sea and from the River to the ends of the earth, we can rest in safety.

For the same reason, we can rejoice at the King's richly furnished table. Like the feasting of Israel in Solomon's time, our feast is a sign of the peace and security we enjoy. Though we may be set upon by numerous enemies, though we may have been deprived of every vine and fig tree, though we may be "resisting to the shedding of blood," when we eat and drink at the Lord's table, we are assured that ultimately nothing can harm us because our Solomon "rules over all the kingdoms."

10
In the Midst of My Enemies

And [Elijah] lay down and slept under a juniper
tree; and behold, there was an angel touching him,
and he said to him, 'Arise, eat' (1 Kings 19:5).

Within the space of two years, three kings had risen and
fallen in Israel. Elah had inherited the throne of his father
Baasha in the twenty-sixth year of Asa, who was ruling at
that time in the Southern kingdom of Judah. Two years
later years, Zimri, a chariot commander, assassinated Elah
while he was getting drunk at Tirzah. The following days
were bloody as Zimri systematically disposed of every remaining member of the house of Baasha, fulfilling the word
of the prophet Jehu. Zimri reigned for only seven days before Omri, the commander of the army, avenged the death
of Elah by attacking Tirzah and overthrowing the short-
lived king. Zimri was burned to death in the king's house
(1 Kings 16:1–20).

After putting down a rebellion led by Tibni, Omri established himself as a powerful ruler. He bought Samaria
and established the capital of Israel on the summit of the
city (1 Kings 16:21–28). To the surrounding nations,
the kingdom of Israel was sometimes referred to as
"Omriland." Peace descended on the war-torn nation, and

Omri's throne was passed without incident to his successor, Ahab. To a casual observer, the kingdom of Israel during the days of Ahab might have seemed the best of times. Certainly it seemed so in comparison with the chaos of the previous generation.

Casual observers, however, are often quite wrong. Despite an appearance of peace and prosperity, the Bible informs us that the period of the Omride dynasty was the worst of times. Omri himself "acted more wickedly than all who were before him," making Israel sin and "provoking Yahweh God of Israel with their idols" (1 Kings 16:25–26). Ahab surpassed his father in wickedness. Not content to follow in the footsteps of Jeroboam I, who initiated calf worship in Israel, Ahab married a princess of Sidon, Jezebel, erected an altar for Baal in Samaria, and set up an Asherah (1 Kings 16:31–33). "Thus," we are told, "Ahab did more to provoke the Lord God of Israel than all the kings of Israel who were before him" (1 Kings 16:33) and "did evil in the sight of the Lord more than all who were before him" (1 Kings 16:30).

In this political and religious situation Elijah suddenly appeared, announcing that the Lord would judge Israel with a drought and call Israel back to her covenant Lord (1 Kings 17:1). As the prophet of a renewed covenant, Elijah was a new Moses, and his life was shaped in many ways by the pattern of Moses' life. Moses fled from Egypt to Midian to get away from Pharaoh; Elijah traveled in the Transjordan to escape Ahab. When Moses returned, he confronted Pharaoh and brought plagues; Elijah confronted Ahab and his "magicians," the prophets of Baal, in the contest on Mount Carmel. Like Moses, Elijah went on a second "exodus," this time traveling as far as Mount Horeb, the very mountain where Moses brought Israel to cut the covenant, and

Yahweh appeared in glory to both Moses and Elijah at Sinai (I Kings 19:1–14).

Unlike Moses, Elijah did not lead a mass exodus. Rather,
as the representative of Israel, Elijah was exiled alone on
Israel's behalf. Since Elijah was the representative Israelite,
the Lord provided food for him in the wilderness, as he had
for Israel. While the Lord withheld rain from the land, He
sustained His prophet by maintaining the brook Cherith
and sending ravens laden with meat and bread (I Kings 17:1–
7). Ravens were unclean birds (Leviticus 11:15), representing Gentile nations, and the Lord thus signified to Elijah
that He would care for him through Gentiles. When the
brook dried up, therefore, Elijah was sent to Zarephath,
near Sidon, to a Gentile widow who had almost nothing
left for herself and her son to eat. Again, the Lord miracu-
lously provided for His prophet, multiplying the widow's
flour and oil so that there was food for them all. This widow,
residing near Sidon (I Kings 17:9), serves as a foil for
Jezebel, princess of Sidon: the widow sustained the prophet's
life, while Jezebel sought to end it. During Elijah's trek
toward Sinai, the Lord again gave food by sending an angel
to provide bread and water (I Kings 19:1–8).

Elijah was not the only one to receive sustenance in
miraculous ways. While the drought destroyed vegetation
and turned Israel into a desert, Obadiah, the God-fearing
steward of Ahab's household, provided bread and water for
one hundred prophets who were living in caves (I Kings
18:5–6). Later, after Micaiah prophesied of Ahab's death
in battle, Ahab sent him to prison to be fed on bread and
water (I Kings 22:27). For all we know, Micaiah remained
in prison for the rest of his life. Even so, the combination
of "bread and water" is so familiar in this section of I Kings
that by the time Micaiah receives them, we know it is a sign

of God's favor to him. Though Ahab and Jezebel devoured the faithful like lions going after their prey, the Lord had kept for Himself a remnant of seven thousand, who had not bowed the knee to Baal, living on "manna and water."

Our God is the same righteous God. Though we may be living in the modern equivalents of catacombs or caves, a greater Obadiah—a "servant of Yah"—continually feeds us. The differences between Elijah's diet and ours, however, should be noted. Bread and water are basic foods, and they were appropriate for the beginning of the new covenant that was brought through Elijah. Bread and water are food and drink for a wilderness people. We, by contrast, are not fed with the sparing rations of the Old Testament prophets—we receive not bread and water, but bread and wine. Wine is not a drink of beginnings but of endings. Wine takes time to produce, and we drink it at the end of the day. Wine is omega, not alpha. That we drink wine at the Lord's table shows that we live after the appearance of the Son who was sent at the "consummation of the ages," in the "fullness of time." In many areas of the world, Ahab still reigns, but the Lord still spreads a table before us in the presence of our enemies. But our table is not only the Lord's care for us; it also signifies that, however rudimentary things may appear to be, in this bread and in this wine, we have tasted the heavenly gift and the powers of the age to come.

11

Sweet Words

> They are more desirable than gold, yes, than much
> fine gold; sweeter also than honey and the drip-
> pings of the honeycomb (Psalm 19:10).

"If any man does not stumble in what he says," James wrote,
"he is a perfect man, able to bridle the whole body as well"
(James 3:1). The tongue is the bit that directs the horse,
the rudder that turns the ship this way and that, the spark
that ignites a forest (vv. 3–6). With these metaphors, James
reinforced the point that controlling the tongue is a test
case of Christian maturity or "perfection." Augustine pointed
to our lack of control over sexual desires and sexual organs
to illustrate the weakness of the human will, but James highlighted our inability to tame the tongue as a sign that we
are not the royal creatures God created us to be. "Every
species of beasts and birds, or reptiles and creatures of the
sea, is tamed" (v. 7), he says, alluding to the creation man-
date of Genesis 1:26–28. But the tongue is "a restless evil
and full of deadly poison," incapable of being tamed. Man
exercises his creative power over all the lower creation, but
is mastered by this small organ. In Paradise, Adam ruled
the beasts with his tongue by naming them; but the sons
of Adam have a wild beast in their own mouths.

One of the key perversions of the tongue is that it is divided: "With it we bless our Lord and Father; and with it we curse men, who have been made in the likeness of God" (v. 9). We are an impossible fountain, which produces both fresh and bitter water; our tongues are fig trees trying with all their might to produce olives (vv. 11–12). Like the serpent, we speak with forked tongues.

In this severe exhortation, James was following a well-known thread of Biblical wisdom, for the book of Proverbs is full of the same warnings. Perverse tongues will be cut out (Proverbs 10:31), and rash speech is like random and wild sword thrusts (12:18); lying tongues have a short life span (12:19), harsh words stir anger (15:1), and fools use their tongues to spout folly (15:2); flattering tongues will not succeed (28:23). Though the Proverbs consistently warn against evil uses of the tongue, they also hold out the possibility that the tongue can be used wisely and even redemptively. Wise tongues are choice silver (10:20) and bring healing (12:18); guarding the tongue is one way of guarding the soul (21:23). Words can be nourishing fruit, and when one uses his tongue wisely, he creates a little Eden around him, complete with a "tree of life" (15:4). Words of the image of God are, like the words of God, powerful for good or ill. Indeed, "death and life are in the hand of the tongue" (Proverbs 18:21).

Thus taming the tongue is a high priority in a Christian's sanctification. But how can this restless evil be reduced to rest? Part of the Bible's answer to this question has to do with the double use of the tongue: we use our tongues to speak, and we use our tongues to taste. Scripture exploits this connection by insisting that the fruit that goes out of our lips is directly connected with the fruit that goes in. We tame our tongues by training our tastes.

Psalm 19 plays off this theme, beginning with a paean to the revelation of God in creation and then turning in verse seven to the praise of God's Word. The Psalmist does not praise God's word for its "intellectual" content so much as its power to transform. God's word has content, but it operates on the whole man, not merely on the brain. It has power to restore souls, wisdom to instruct the simple, light for the blind, joy for the faint-hearted. For all these reasons and more, the judgments and statutes of Yahweh are better than gold, tastier than the sweetest honey. The Word of Yahweh is not only a standard for all truth (though it is that), not only a moral and ethical guide for all life (though it is that, too). It is also food, and only when we come to delight in its sweetness do we receive the Word as we should.

After enumerating the wonders of God's Word, David ends the Psalm by requesting, "May the words of my mouth and the meditation of my heart be acceptable in Thy sight, O Yahweh" (v. 14). This prayer would only be answered if the law of Yahweh was to David what David said it was—perfect, sure, pure, clean, true, desirable, sweet. Only when we come to delight in the taste of God's Word are we able to produce words that are acceptable, tasty, to God. Like the prophets, if we are to speak rightly, we must first eat the book, and we must learn to enjoy it.

At least since Augustine, the sacraments have been understood as "visible words." James Jordan has suggested that the Supper is more appropriately called an "edible word," but even so the analogy of Word and Sacrament stands. This notion of sacramental "words" picks up on the thread of imagery we have been examining here, that is, the biblical connection between receiving God's Word and eating it. Paul makes it clear that the celebration of the Supper is, in some manner, a proclamation of the death of Christ, an act of preaching (1 Corinthians 11:26). The Supper is the gospel made food, and in this transformation of proclamation into meal, the Supper replicates the history of Jesus Himself: Jesus is the "Word made flesh," and in becoming flesh, His flesh has become living and life-giving bread, our manna in the wilderness (John 6:41–59). Word became flesh so that He might become our food.

Receiving the "visible word" of God at the Lord's table is thus part of the process of sanctification, the development of good taste. As our "rudder" is trained, the whole ship will come under control. One way that the Supper trains our tongues is by training them for praise. Historically, "Eucharist" has been one of the names assigned to the Lord's Supper, used not only by high church theologians but also occasionally by Calvin and more frequently by Zwingli. "Eucharist" means "thanksgiving," and the Supper takes this name from the prayers of thanksgiving Jesus offered before breaking bread and distributing wine. Though thanksgiving is not all that is going on at the Lord's Table, it is going on at the Lord's table, and as we join again and again together in "Eucharist" for the gifts of bread and wine, we are being trained to use our tongues for thanksgiving. We celebrate the Eucharist in part so that we may learn, as the Book of Common Prayer puts it, to give thanks to Him "at all times and in all places."

Nothing is automatic here. Some have so dulled their taste that the sweet bread of heaven will be bitter herbs. For those who come to the table seeking Christ, however, the Supper is, like the Word, honey in the honeycomb, and the invitation remains: "Taste, and see that the Lord is good."

12

Lady Wisdom's Banquet

Wisdom has built her house, she has hewn out her
seven pillars; she has prepared her food, she has mixed
her wine; she has also set her table (Proverbs
9:1–2).

The opening chapters of Proverbs present three main characters: Lady Folly and Lady Wisdom, both of whom are
seeking to catch the interest of the young man who is the
focus of the book. Wisdom calls out to "naive ones" who
"love simplicity" and urges them accept her reproof, receive her spirit, and hear her words (1:20–23). Lady Folly
is a prostitute, boisterous and rebellious, who invites the
young man to her bed to "drink our fill of love until morning" and "delight ourselves with caresses" (7:6–23). Choosing between the ladies is choosing between life and death.
Calamity will come on those who refuse Wisdom "like a
whirlwind" (1:27), for Lady Folly is leading the young man
like an ox to slaughter (7:22–23). Whoever embraces Wisdom, however, finds life (8:35).

In Proverbs 9, this contrast of Wisdom and Folly comes
to its climax, as each of the ladies spreads a table and en-
tices the young man to share a meal. Folly calls on the streets
with the promise that "stolen water is sweet; and bread in

secret is pleasant" (9:17). Earlier, Lady Folly has enticed the young man with similar promises: "I was due to offer peace offerings"— which means that she has plenty of fresh meat to offer—and she offers an invitation to "drink our fill of love until morning" (7:14, 18). Wisdom likewise sets a table in her house, complete with mixed wine, and invites the young man to eat and drink with her. There is a table of Wisdom and a table of Folly. There is a table of the Lord and a table of demons.

Culinary and sexual temptations are interwoven in the speech of Lady Folly, a combination of imagery that is not unique to this passage. In the Song of Songs, the bridegroom is "like an apple tree among the trees of the forest," whose "fruit was sweet to my taste." At his banquet hall he offers raisin cakes and apples, but the banquet hall is really his bedroom where "his left hand is under my head, and his right hand embraces me" (Song of Songs 2:3–6). From the bridegroom's perspective, the bride's love is "better than wine" and her lips "drip honey." She is a promised land, with "honey and milk" under her tongue; she is like an orchard of pomegranates, a fruitful garden fed by a spring of fresh water (Song of Songs 4:7–15). Lady Folly's offer is a perverse form of Solomon's banquet of love. Like the bride and groom in the Song of Songs, she is not only offering food and drink. She is offering *herself* as food and drink.

This linkage of sex and food, which is common not only in Scripture but in much literature and religion, is part of the design of creation. Sexual intercourse is a physical union of a man and woman into one flesh, and sexual passion is passion for this intimate union. A shared meal, as James Jordan has explained, forms a similar relationship among those who eat together. Everyone at the table eats from one roast, one loaf, one casserole dish, and as they consume a common portion of food, they are bound together in a "one-flesh" relationship. Paul recognized this reality when he said that sharing a common loaf makes us "one body" (1 Corinthians 10:17), just as a man who has sex with a prostitute is "one body" with her (1 Corinthians 6:15–16). Communion is our "marriage Supper" with the Lamb, the meal in which we receive Christ's flesh that joins us to our Husband as one flesh.

Wisdom, Solomon's words suggest, is acquired at the dinner table, as much as in the study or the library, as we cling to Lady Wisdom and share her food. Figuratively, this means that we are to chew and digest every crumb we can receive from her, consuming her words so that they become bone of our bone and flesh of our flesh. What we "eat" has a direct effect on our spiritual health. This was the ethical message of the laws concerning clean and unclean animals in the Old Testament: we have to be careful about what we take in, because we are what we eat. More literally, since bad company corrupts good morals, Solomon is telling us that acquiring wisdom demands that we choose our companions carefully—"companion" intended here in the etymological sense of "those who share bread."

Of course, these passages about Lady Wisdom point to Jesus, who, Paul tells us, is the "power of God and the wisdom of God" (1 Corinthians 1:24), "in whom are hidden all the treasures of wisdom and knowledge" (Colossians 2:3). At His table, He has prepared His food and mixed His wine, and as the Wisdom of God, He calls in the streets for us to join him at the "banquet of Wisdom." The gospel invitation is an invitation to a banquet, which includes intimate fellowship and communication of wisdom. Choosing wise table fellows will make us wise, but accepting this invitation, the marriage proposal of Wisdom Himself, makes us wise unto salvation.

In Proverbs, Wisdom is a woman, and that suggests a further dimension to Solomon's portrait of Wisdom's banquet. Typologically, it is not only Jesus Himself who calls us to share the banquet of Wisdom, but His bride, the church. As we share table fellowship with Him, we are also sharing table fellowship with her, and joined in one body with her who is one body with Christ, we grow in wisdom, in order to grow into Wisdom.

13

Wine on the Lees

And the Lord of hosts will prepare a lavish banquet
for all peoples on this mountain; a banquet of aged
wine, choice pieces with marrow, and refined, aged
wine (Isaiah 25:6).

Nietzsche began his *Birth of Tragedy* by contrasting the
Apollonian and Dionysian motifs in Greek life. Apollo represented reason and order, and the Apollonian side of the
Greek character was manifested in sculpture, with its smooth
lines and placid faces. Dionysus was the god of disorder,
of revelry and wine, and drama was the art that best displayed the Dionysian side of the Hellenistic character.

Of these two, most Christians would readily associate
the God of Scripture with Apollo—for God is infinite,
eternal, and unchangeable, without body, parts or passions.
This, however, was not the view of some ancient writers.
Plutarch, through a series of imaginative associations, concluded that the God of the Jews was not Apollo, but
Dionysus. "The Jews themselves," Plutarch wrote, "testify
to a connection with Dionysus when they keep the Sabbath by inviting each other to drink and to enjoy wine;
when more important business interferes with this custom,
they regularly take at least a sip of neat wine." That

Yahweh is the true God of wine is evident in many places in Scripture. Jesus' first miracle was to transform water into wine at the wedding of Canaan, and Psalm 104 says that Yahweh is the One who makes wine to gladden the heart of man.

The prophecy in Isaiah 25 further illustrates this theme. Isaiah prophesied in the Southern kingdom while the Assyrians were arising from the East and threatening Israel and Judah. Early in his prophecy, he condemned the kings of Judah for relying on alliances with the surrounding nations for protection against the encroaching Assyrians, but the pressure on the Southern kings was great. Israel, led by Pekah, had joined with the Arameans under Rezin to force Judah to join an anti-Assyrian alliance. Pekah and Rezin agreed, "Let us go up against Judah and terrorize it" (Isaiah 7:6). Isaiah reminded Ahaz, then king in Jerusalem, that "the head of Aram is Damascus and the head of Damascus is Rezin" and told Ahaz that "the head of Ephraim is Samaria and the head of Samaria is the son of Remaliah" (7:8–9). This hardly seems encouraging, until we realize that Ahaz was supposed to finish the series of equations: "The head of Judah is Jerusalem and the head of Jerusalem is . . . Yahweh." If Ahaz remembered this and lived by faith in Yahweh's deliverance, he would be saved. If instead he turned elsewhere for help—to Egypt, for example—there would be no support.

The threat of invasion and the need to rely on Yahweh's help is also the theme of the stories that are found at the center of Isaiah's prophecy. Chapters 36–39 describe the Assyrian threat to Jerusalem during the reign of Hezekiah, the son of Ahaz. In his fourteenth year, the Assyrians got to the walls of Jerusalem but were repelled when the Lord sent His angel to kill 185,000 Assyrians in their camp. It was another Passover, and the city was saved. Shortly after, Hezekiah foolishly welcomed a delegation of visitors from Babylon and showed them the riches of the temple. As a result, the Lord said that He would someday bring Babylon back to Jerusalem to carry away "all that your fathers have laid up in store to this day" (39:6). This looming exile in Babylon is in the background through the rest of Isaiah, and it is the setting for all the wonderful promises of salvation found in those chapters. For Isaiah, the salvation of Israel would be chiefly their return from exile in a new exodus, their reconquest of the land, and the restoration of Eden in the land of promise.

This setting of exile and return, which pervades the whole book, helps us to understand the promises of Isaiah 25. The "mountain" in verse seven is Mount Zion, which is the same as the "mountain of the house of the Lord" in Isaiah 2:2. In the "latter days," that is, after the exile, the Lord promised to exalt Zion as the chief of the mountains, and not only Israel but the nations would stream to it to be taught of the Lord. At the same mountain, the Lord promised to prepare a banquet of wine (25:6) celebrating Judah's return, a return that would be Israel's resurrection from the dead (see Ezekiel 37). Judah had been under a sentence of death because of her sins—scattered among the nations. But the Lord promised that the "covering" of death that had hovered over Judah would be swallowed up, their reproach would be removed, and the tears of Judah would be turned to rejoicing (25:8–9). Death devours men, but the Lord promised to devour the devourer. The feast on the Lord's mountain, then, celebrates both the return from exile and the Lord's victory over death. Or rather, it celebrates the return from exile *as* the Lord's victory over death.

Like the feast of the returned Israelites, the Lord's Supper celebrates our return from exile. Adam was exiled from God's presence because of his sin, but Jesus bore our exile on the cross, the exile of being forsaken by His Father. Because He has endured the curse of exile, we are enabled to return, and celebrate this feast of wine at a heavenly Zion (see Hebrews 12). This meal is also a celebration of Christ's victory over death. His death swallowed up death and tore away the covering that had been stretched out over us; the devourer is devoured because Jesus was devoured.

Isaiah's prophecy thus foretold not only the restoration of Israel but the restoration of the nations. As Isaiah saw it, the gospel invitation was an invitation not only to learn from the law of the Lord, but an invitation to a feast flowing with abundant wine, as well as rich meats. As Isaiah saw it, God would someday work to bring deliverance to all nations, and by this would prove Himself before all nations to be the true God of the vine.

14

Zealous for His Land

> Then I will make up to you for the years that the
> swarming locust has eaten, the creeping locust, the
> stripping locust, and the gnawing locust, My great
> army which I sent among you. And you shall have
> plenty to eat and be satisfied (Joel 2:25–26a).

Joel's prophecy famously focuses on a locust plague, a dev-astating judgment in the Ancient Near East. Instead of a lightsome cloud of winged cherubim spreading out over the land, Israel got winged locusts, a dark and demonic glory-cloud. Four different types of locusts covered the land (1:4), stretching to the four corners and devastating everything in their way. Unlike the glory-cloud, which hovered over creation and brought order and life, the locust cloud brought destruction and death wherever it went.

Specifically, the locust plague deprived Israel of food. Whatever one type of locust left behind was eaten up by the next wave (1:4) so that the land, which had stretched out like a fruitful garden before the locusts, was a desolate wilderness behind them (2:3). Drunkards wept because there was no wine (1:5). Fields were ruined and grain dried up (1:10). Farmers and vinedressers were devastated (1:11), their vines and trees without fruit (1:12). Even lions went

hungry and thirsty as the "fire" of locusts burned the land
(1:16–20). Worst of all, Israel could not continue her
worship of Yahweh because they had no grain offerings or
libations in the house of God from Sabbath to Sabbath
(1:9). The locusts not only left the family table empty
but took food from the table of the Lord. Feasting had
come to an end, but, more tragically, "gladness and joy"
were cut off "from the house of our God" (1:16). Since
this worship was the means by which Israel maintained fellowship with her covenant King and Lord, the famine had
catastrophic liturgical consequences. No food in Israel meant
that the nation was threatened, and no food in Israel meant
that her status as God's people was threatened.

In response to this crisis, Joel called on the people to
fast—appropriately enough, since by fasting they were agree-
ing with God's judgment that had deprived them of food.
Perhaps, he said, the Lord might relent and restore a grain
offering and libation. If the people mourned and fasted and
rent their hearts, the Lord might restore the gracious ministry of the temple (2:15–17).

And the Lord did respond. Immediately after the fast
was called, Joel told the people that the "Lord will be zealous for His land" (2:18). This is the key transition in the
prophecy for, after this point, all the devastating effects
of the locust plague began to be reversed: the flood waters
began to recede when God remembered His people. Having described the judgment as a loss of food, Joel celebrated
the restoration as a return to fruitfulness and plenty. Yahweh promised to give rain (2:23), so that the "threshing
floors will be full of grain, and the vats will overflow with
the new wine and oil" (2:24). What the locusts had eaten
would be restored, so that "you shall have plenty to eat and
be satisfied" (2:25–26a). Israel would enter into Sabbath

rest from her enemies. This was not only a restoration of material prosperity but a restoration to God's favor. Temple worship would begin again, and Israel would know that the Lord was in their midst and that He was their God (2:27). The final verses of Joel promised an Edenic abundance and richness: "The mountains will drip with sweet wine, and the hills will flow with milk, and the brooks will flow with water, and a spring will go out from the house of the Lord" (3:18).

Israel's restoration was also her "vindication" (2:23). The word for "vindication" in Hebrew is a word related to "judge," and it means that Yahweh has passed a judgment in favor of His people and made that judgment public before the world by restoring their prosperity. In short, "vindication" is virtually the same term as the New Testament term "justification," which also refers to the Lord's favorable judgment. In Joel, the restoration of Israel's prosperity was her "vindication," because this displayed before the nations that Yahweh had kept faith with His people Israel. The fact that Israel once again ate and drank the Lord's abundant provision was a sign that the Lord had declared her "not guilty." Eating and drinking in the Lord's presence declared that there was no condemnation, that those who gathered at this table were justified in His sight, that the Lord had driven away the cloud of locusts that had darkened the land.

In this context Joel made his prophecy about the outpouring of the Spirit. The gift of the Spirit was one part of a complex set of events that included the Lord's vindication of Israel, the restoration of her prosperity, and judgment on the Gentiles who had fought against her (3:1–8). When Peter quoted from this prophecy in Acts 2, all of this hope was coming into play, and the good news that

Peter proclaimed was that all these promises had been fulfilled. The true Israel was raised up in Jesus, the Lord by
the Spirit was now coming to dwell among them, and the
nations were going to be shaken and harvested.

It was no accident, then, that the converts on Pentecost immediately began communing together at the table
in the "breaking of bread" (Acts 2:42). Joel's prophecy
had been fulfilled, and that meant that the devastating and
devouring "locusts" had been thrust back, the Spirit poured
out, and the earth made fruitful. The meal of the early church
celebrated the restoration of Israel, her resurrection as a
new Israel. Feasting in God's presence was a sign that, by
faith in the crucified and risen Jesus, they were "vindicated,"
judged righteous before the Lord. It was a sign that the
Lord had "been zealous for His land" and had restored to
her grain, new wine, and oil.

15

New Covenant, New Meal

'And I will fill the soul of the priests with abundance, and My people will be satisfied with My goodness,' declares the Lord (Jeremiah 31:14).

Since the time of Joshua, Israel's settlement in the land had been one of the chief symbols of Israel's identity. Yahweh had promised the land to Abraham, and Israel's possession of it was a sign that she was truly the people of Abraham, heir to all the promises made to him. Yet through much of her history, Israel's hold on the land was tenuous. During the period of the judges, enemy nations moved in and took control of the land, and when Assyria began to expand from the east, Israel's possession of the land was threatened.

Jeremiah lived in Jerusalem during the last days of the kingdom of Judah. Nebuchadnezzar's Babylonian empire was expanding into Judah's territory until Jerusalem itself, the city of Yahweh and of David, was besieged. Given the importance of the land and the city in Israel's history and her consciousness, many Jews were understandably determined to fight to the bitter end to retain the land. Jeremiah, however, offered a very different program: "Surrender to Babylon, go peaceably into exile, and once you get to Babylon, promote the welfare and peace of the city that has conquered you" (Jeremiah 29:1–14). To many Jews, this was as much as to say, "Give up thinking of yourselves as the people of Abraham." No wonder many thought that Jeremiah must be a Babylonian sympathizer, a traitor to Judah.

In fact, Jeremiah's attack on the hotheads in Judah was not the act of a traitor, but the far-sightedness of a wise man loyal to the people of God. Jeremiah was grievously tortured by the prospect that Judah would lose possession of the land and go into exile, and this attitude is reflected in his prayers, which are among the most intense in the Bible. Though Jeremiah labored passionately for the good of Judah, he realized that preserving the people of Judah meant that she must give up her political independence. If Judah tried to hold out against Nebuchadnezzar, she would be crushed. If, on the other hand, she surrendered, she would be exiled and subjected to a foreign power, but the nation would survive. The tree of Israel may be cut down, but from that stump, Jeremiah was sure, Yahweh would cause new branches to grow. Gloom would descend on the land, but the Creator would speak again to call light out of the darkness.

Jeremiah urged the people to surrender to Babylon also because he knew that the exile would not be permanent. In the very passage where he commanded the exiles to settle in and pursue the welfare of Babylon, he predicted that the exile would last seventy years (Jeremiah 29:10)—a long time to be away from home, but not forever. Jeremiah ended his book with a prediction of the eventual fall of Babylon. Confident that the Lord would remove Babylon from the scene, the Jews could submit to Nebuchadnezzar without fear. There was no need for Judah to cling ferociously to her rights; in time, the Lord would protect and vindicate those who trusted Him and bring Sabbath rest to His people.

Jeremiah, in short, was not only a prophet of exile, but a prophet who foresaw a return from exile. The same Lord who carried Israel on eagle's wings from Egypt would do the same to bring His people from Babylon. As Jeremiah described it, however, the return from exile would be more than a geographic move. It would bring in a new covenant, a covenant superior to the covenant that the Lord had made through Moses: "Behold, days are coming, declares the Lord, when I will make a new covenant with the house of Israel and with the house of Judah, not like the covenant which I made with their fathers in the day I took them by the hand to bring them out of the land of Egypt." In this new covenant, the Lord promised to "put My law within them, and on their heart I will write it; and I will be their God, and they shall be my people" (Jeremiah 31:31–33).

In one crucial respect, the new covenant would be like the old: in both, God promised to give land. After the exile, the One who had "scattered Israel will gather him, and keep him as a shepherd keeps his flock" (31:10). As in the covenant at Sinai, the gift of land was the gift of food: "And they shall come and shout for joy on the height of Zion, and they shall be radiant over the bounty of the Lord— over the grain, and the new wine, and the oil, and over the young of the herd and of the flock" (31:12). The returned exiles would dance with joy, as the Lord restored Eden in their midst, for "their life shall be like a watered garden" (31:12). Priests and people would be satisfied with the "fatness" of the Lord's gift.

Israel returned to the land, and the nation was restored under the leadership of Joshua and Zerubbabel, Ezra and Nehemiah. Great as this restoration was, however, it left Israel hoping for a far greater fulfillment. Centuries passed, until on a spring evening in Jerusalem, a young rabbi passed a cup of wine to his disciples and declared that this wine was "the new covenant in My blood" (Luke 22:20). Jesus was saying that in Him Yahweh was accomplishing what He had promised Israel through Jeremiah. And the sign of this fulfillment was a meal of bread and wine. In this feast, we declare the accomplished fact that, in Christ, we have returned from exile; that we have been filled with the fatness of the earth; that we have been restored to a well-watered garden. For this is the blood of the new covenant.

16

The Good Shepherd

'And I will feed [my sheep] in a good pasture, and
their grazing ground will be on the mountain heights
of Israel. There they will lie down in good grazing
ground, and they will feed in rich pasture on the
mountains of Israel. I will feed My flock and I will
lead them to rest,' declares the Lord God (Ezekiel
34:14–15).

When Christians hear the word "pastor," they think of a
leader, a "shepherd," in the church. This is as it should be,
because the Greek equivalents of "pastor" are applied to
the church's leaders in the New Testament (see Ephesians
4:11). Throughout the Old Testament, however, a "pastor" or "shepherd" is not a religious but a political leader.
Israel's "pastors" were her kings, not her priests. When
Jeremiah pronounced a woe against the "shepherds who are
destroying and scattering the sheep of My pasture" (23:1),
it was part of an attack on the abuses of Judah's royal family (see 22:1). In place of the oppressive shepherds, the
Lord promised to raise up "for David a righteous Branch,
and he will reign as king and act wisely and do justice and
righteousness in the land" (23:5). Ezekiel 34 has the same
focus: it is a prophecy against the "shepherds of Israel,"
that is, the kings.

Ezekiel had been taken east to Babylon in one of the deportations of Nebuchadnezzar, and the early chapters of his prophecy cover the same time period as the book of Jeremiah. Jerusalem and its temple were still standing, but while in Babylon Ezekiel received word that Nebuchadnezzar had taken the city (33:21–22). These events back home had a direct effect on Ezekiel's ministry. Earlier, when Ezekiel's wife had died, the Lord had instructed the prophet not to show any sign of mourning for his wife, "the desire of your eyes, and the delight of your soul" (24:21–24). Silence was imposed on Ezekiel until Jerusalem fell. Of course, Ezekiel's silence was not total. We do not have a long blank section in our Bibles from Ezekiel 24–33. Throughout this time, Ezekiel prophesied about the coming desolation on the nations surrounding Jerusalem, but toward Judah, he maintained utter silence.

When he finally did open his mouth again, he began prophesying of the restoration of the people of God. Judah, Ezekiel promised, would be given a new spirit (chapter 36), and would be raised up from the death of exile and reunited with her sister Israel (chapter 37). Formed into an exceedingly great army by the power of the Word and Spirit, Judah would be victorious in a great international war (chapters 38–39), rebuild the temple, redivide the land, which would be transformed into a garden by the water flowing from the temple (chapters 40–48). Though chastened by exile, she would someday be restored to her former glory as the true Adamic people.

Restoration of righteous leadership was part of the promise of Israel's renewal, and this is what Ezekiel 34 is about. In large part, the chapter is a condemnation of the past and present shepherds of Judah. They have not strengthened the weak, healed the sick, bound up the broken, or

gathered the sheep who had "wandered through all the mountains and on every high hill" and been "scattered over all
the surface of the earth" (34:4–6). Much of the imagery
of the passage has to do with food. False shepherds "feed
themselves" rather than feeding the flock (v. 3), and their
negligence had left the sheep vulnerable to the beasts of
the field, savage nations that swooped down on the flock
like an eagle to its prey (v. 28). Yahweh of hosts, however,
promised to stand against these shepherds "because My flock
has become a prey, My flock has even become food for all
the beasts of the field for lack of a shepherd, and My shepherds did not search for the flock, but rather the shepherds fed themselves and did not feed the flock" (34:8–10).
False shepherds slaughter and devour the sheep, feeding on
them rather than feeding them.

Ezekiel also delivered the Lord's promise of a good
shepherd, who would do for Israel all the things that the
evil shepherds had failed to do. He would "deliver them
from all the places to which they were scattered on a cloudy
and gloomy day" (v. 12) and would "seek the lost, bring
back the scattered, bind up the broken, and strengthen the
sick" (v. 16). Above all, the good shepherd would feed his
flock, leading them to "good pasture, and their grazing
ground will be on the mountain heights of Israel" (v. 14).
Judah would someday graze in safety, lying down "in good
grazing ground" and feeding "in rich pasture" (v. 14). For
their part, the false shepherds would also receive their appropriate portion: the good shepherd threatened to "feed
them with judgment" (v. 16).

Such wonderful things could only be accomplished by
Yahweh Himself, and He promised to pastor His people:
"I Myself will search for My sheep and seek them out" (v.
11), and "I, even I, will judge between the fat sheep and the

lean sheep" (v. 20). Yet, Yahweh also promised that He would send another David to shepherd His people: "I will set over them one shepherd, My servant David, and he will feed them; he will feed them himself and be their shepherd" (v. 23).

Jesus is this "Good Shepherd" (John 10:11). He is the promised son of David, who is also Yahweh Himself appearing in flesh. Jesus is not like the shepherds of Israel, the Pharisees and scribes, who stuffed themselves with the flesh of the sheep, warmed themselves with their wool, and devoured the flock or left them to wolves. Jesus is the Good Shepherd. He does not force the sheep to serve Him but instead lays down His life for them. Jesus is the Good Shepherd. To the scattered and lost sheep of Israel, to the devoured and feeble, Jesus issued an invitation to follow Him, the true shepherd of the house of Israel. Jesus is the Good Shepherd. Exalted now above the firmament, He invites us to a meal, a meal where the sick are healed, the broken bound up, the weak strengthened. He offers His flesh and blood as true food and drink. He invites us to rich pastures, green beside still waters.

17
A Place at the Table

> Daniel made up his mind that he would not defile himself with the king's choice food or with the wine which he drank (Daniel 1:8).

Modest though it is as a political slogan, "We just want a place at the table" has become the guiding principle for much of the Religious Right. Uninspiring rhetoric such as this is, in part, a conscious effort to soothe secularists who are spooked by even the most modest gesture toward public religion; even the simple addition of "In God We Trust" seems to them to pollute coins that bear the American eagle. But the slogan and the attitude it embodies also illustrate the widespread Christian acceptance of liberal political order, an order in which there is only one rule governing access to political power: anyone can have a place at the table so long as he renounces any effort to take over the table. As Stanley Fish has put it, Christian activists and political theorists who agree to play by this rule have become adepts at "playing not to win."

Seeking a place at the table is attractive partly because it seems achievable. When you play not to win, failure is success. But even playing not to win has its own temptations, as the story of Daniel and his friends in Babylon implies. This story provides a model for faithfulness in the midst of unbelief that we do well to examine afresh; it shows us a group of Jews that plays to win, but whose paradoxical tactics look more like refusing to play at all.

As a young man, Daniel found himself in Babylon, the capital city of the greatest world empire of the day. Innate intelligence and handsome appearance won him a coveted spot at the "university" of Babylon where he was trained in all the literature and language of the Chaldeans, in preparation for entering the king's service (Daniel 1:1–5). It was an enviable opportunity for a young foreigner. Nebuchadnezzar, like Eve, saw something pleasing to the eyes which was able to supply wisdom; he picked these choice young men from the vine of Israel. As it turned out, he got more than he knew, for the wisdom that came from this fruit far transcended anything that Babylonian wisdom could provide (see Daniel 2).

Daniel and his friends, though picked by Nebuchadnezzar to be the king's servants, also knew that they remained servants of Yahweh, King of Israel. Nebuchadnezzar was hoping that the four young men would be consumed with his service, and they had to resist the temptation to forget the King in their service to the king. Their battle with Nebuchadnezzar took place on two symbolic fronts. First, Daniel and his friends were all given new names, Babylonian equivalents for their given Hebrew names. Each of their Hebrew names included a name of God (Daniel 1:6; "El" means "God," and "Iah" is a form of "Yahweh"), and their Babylonian names all referred to Babylonian gods. Here, the battle was about their identity: which name manifested who they really were? Would they name themselves by Yahweh or by some idol?

The other area of conflict had to do with food. Quite

literally, Daniel had won a place at the table of the most powerful ruler of his time. But Daniel had already determined that he would not defile himself with "the king's choice food or with the wine which he drank" (1:8). It is not clear why the king's food was defiling. There is no hint that the food was unclean according to the standards of Leviticus 11 and Deuteronomy 14; nothing is said in the text about unclean fish or birds. Even if the food had been sacrificed to idols, as some have suggested, it would not have been sinful to eat it (see 1 Corinthians 8). Daniel, it seems, did not refuse the king's food because there was anything particularly wrong with the food, but because of the more general symbolism of sharing a table. To eat with someone, to share his food, is to be united and bonded with him. Daniel and his friends would eventually become servants of Nebuchadnezzar, but they wished to make it clear at the outset that their ultimate King and Master was not the Babylonian emperor, but the Lord of heaven and earth who ruled the eastern land of Babylon as well as Israel's land toward the sunset. Whatever food they shared with Nebuchadnezzar, they were first of all table companions of another King.

These young men from Judah were surely surrounded by ambitious young Babylonians, all using their access to the king to increase their access to the king. To such colleagues, it must have seemed that Daniel and his friends wanted to lose, as their odd religious scruples endangered what minimal access they achieved. But Daniel knew what he was doing. Instead of taking the king's food, Daniel, significantly, asked for "seeds" (1:12; not "vegetables," as in many translations). Daniel and his friends formed the cornerstones of a new house of Israel, an Israel that would endure the Babylonian exile and return to the land. From these "seeds" Israel would spring up anew, and so asking for "seeds" was an appropriate symbol of their moment in history. Eating seeds was, moreover, the corollary of refusing Nebuchadnezzar's food. Daniel and his friends could only be the "seeds" of a new Israel if they held themselves aloof from the king's table. Had they compromised with Nebuchadnezzar, they would have produced thorns and thistles; by devoting themselves to Yahweh, they ensured that Israel, once replanted in her homeland, would flourish with grass producing seed and fruit trees with their seed in them. To all appearances, they were refusing to follow the rules of political advancement, but what looked like "playing to lose" was, in fact, the opposite. Daniel knew that advancement does not come from east or west, but from the Lord of heaven, and it was Daniel, not one of his assertive Babylonian counterparts, who eventually rose to become the third ruler of Babylon.

Jesus said that we cannot serve two masters, and Paul applied this principle to table fellowship when he said that we cannot partake of the table of the Lord and the table of demons (1 Corinthians 10:21). The mere fact that "tables of demons" exist should make us cautious about adopting an agenda whose goal is to secure a place at a table. However strategic it may seem, acquiring a place at the table of demons never advances God's kingdom, and it is a betrayal of the confession we make when we sit at the Lord's table.

Not every king is demonic, of course, but even if we should enter service to a righteous king, we must always insist that our primary loyalty is to Jesus. And we must always remember that this is a meal memorializing the *crucified* Jesus, who died as a victim of the combined injustice of Jerusalem and Rome. Christians who feast at *this* table with understanding cannot be naive about the realities of power and its many abuses. Christians who feast at this table will know that playing to win sometimes means that we must refuse a place at the table.

18

From Temple to City: From Passover to Booths

> And the entire assembly of those who had returned from the captivity made booths and lived in them. The sons of Israel had indeed not done so from the days of Joshua the son of Nun to that day. And there was great rejoicing (Nehemiah 8:17).

Cities are eschatological. That is to say, a city takes time to build and is, as Lewis Mumford put it, time and human effort made permanently visible in buildings, monuments, and wide avenues. Scripturally too, cities come at the end of things. Israel's history moved from a rural-based civilization during the period of the judges toward a more urban civilization under David and Solomon, and the whole sweep of biblical history progresses from a garden to the city of God.

When the Jews exiled of Babylon returned, they recognized that the goal was not simply to resettle the land but to rebuild the city of Jerusalem, and with it the more urban culture that characterized the monarchical period. After seventy years of exile, Cyrus the Persian let Israel go back from the east to her own land, giving instructions that they were to "build a house in Jerusalem," the "house of

Yahweh, the God of Israel" (Ezra 1:1–4). As Ezra-Nehemiah progresses, however, it becomes clear that the goal of the restoration people was not only to build the temple but to build Jerusalem itself into the "house of Yahweh, the God of Israel."

But cities are eschatological; the Jews did not begin with rebuilding the city. Instead, led by the High Priest Joshua and Zerubbabel, a descendant of David, they worked to reestablish the altar. During the first year after the return, in the seventh month, the altar was set up and the cycle of offerings laid out in Numbers 28–29 was reinstituted (see Ezra 3:1–7). After the altar came the temple, and in the second year, the cornerstone of the temple was laid with much rejoicing (3:10–11). Work had begun quickly, but the rapid progress did not continue. Enemies of Israel protested to the king of Persia that if the Jews were allowed to erect the house of the Lord, they would begin to rebel against the empire. Israel's history of rebellion against Babylon provided plenty of support to their suspicions, so the Persians put an end to the rebuilding (Ezra 4:1–24).

Spurred by the preaching of the prophets Haggai and Zechariah, Joshua, Zerubbabel and the people eventually returned to building and even received Darius's confirmation of their legal right to proceed. Four years later, on the third day of the month Adar around the time of Passover, the temple was completed. At the full moon, Israel celebrated Passover in her new temple on the fourteenth day of the month and then observed the week-long feast of Unleavened Bread, "for Yahweh caused them to rejoice, and had turned the heart of the king of Assyria toward them to encourage them in the work of the house of God, the God of Israel" (6:22).

Passover and Unleavened Bread, feasts of the first month, celebrated the new beginning of Israel after her new exodus. Passover originally celebrated Israel's birth out of Egypt, and during the feast of Unleavened Bread, old leaven was cut off to make way for new. These feasts, as celebrations of origins, were appropriate festivals to mark the completion of the temple. Just as Solomon's temple was the endpoint of the Exodus (see 1 Kings 6:1), so in the same way the building of the second temple was the endpoint of the "second exodus" from Babylon. Yahweh of hosts had raised Israel from the dead to shine like stars in the heavens, and in their celebration of Unleavened Bread, they cut off the old leaven of Babylon and began with the new leaven of the restoration.

Though Passover and Unleavened Bread celebrated the completion of the exodus, the exodus was only the beginning of Israel's restoration. These festivals celebrate the end of the beginning, but not the final goal of Israel's rebirth. Thus, after Joshua and Zerubbabel completed the temple, the city was still in ruins, and Nehemiah had to come to lead the people in restoring its walls and gates. Further labor, and additional celebration, were yet to come.

After much opposition and trial, Israel, under Nehemiah's leadership, restored the city of Jerusalem, and, having completed that work, Israel again celebrated, this time the Feast of Booths (Nehemiah 8:13–18). Booths memorialized Israel's wandering in the wilderness, when Israel was forced to live in "booths," but it was also a harvest feast, celebrating the ingathering of the wheat in the seventh month. As the feast of "ingathering," Booths was a feast that celebrated the "end of the end" and not merely the "end of the beginning." It anticipated the harvest of the nations, God's gathering His own into His barns. It looked to the "harvest at the end of the age."

In the feasts of Passover and Booths and in the progression that occurs between them, we have a window on
the progress of redemptive history. History move from
the new beginnings of Unleavened Bread toward a final harvest. Unleavened bread cuts off old leaven and introduced
new leaven, and at Booths, the people of God rejoice that
the new leaven has leavened the whole loaf. From the view
of Ezra-Nehemiah, another perspective overlays this: history moves from the building of a temple to the building
of a city. Passover and Unleavened bread celebrate the erection
of the temple; Booths looks to the throngs who will popu-
late the city of God.

This double perspective—from planting to harvest,
from temple to city—comes to a single focal point in the
Lord's Supper, for the Lord's Supper is our Passover and
our feast of Unleavened Bread. "Christ our Passover has
been sacrificed," Paul wrote, and this immediately follows
an exhortation to "clean out the old leaven" and is followed
by a further exhortation to celebrate the feast, the Christian Passover, "not with old leaven, nor with the leaven of
malice and wickedness, but with the unleavened bread of
sincerity and truth" (1 Corinthians 5:7–8). Because the
definitive Passover Lamb has been sacrificed, we are in a
perpetual feast of Unleavened Bread, continually cutting
off the old leaven. In Christ, there has been a new and even
greater exodus, which we celebrate at the His table. In Him,
a new temple has been established, for He, together with
His body, is a temple of the Spirit.

But the Supper is also our Feast of Booths, and that
means that the Supper is not only a temple celebration but
a civic festival. In His resurrection, Christ is the "firstfruits"
of the harvest (1 Corinthians 15:23), and the outpouring
of the Spirit brings in the "first loaf" at Pentecost

(Acts 2; Leviticus 23). The full harvest is yet to be gathered, but it will certainly occur, for the firstfruits of the harvest is a pledge of the full harvest; just so, the city is not yet completed, but we celebrate because the Jesus is a greater Nehemiah who is building a city, a city that is truly eschatological. At this table, we celebrate the present reality and anticipate the future fullness of a city that comes down out of heaven.

19

The Cup of the Lord

Then Mordecai recorded these events, and he sent
letters to all the Jews who were in all the provinces
of King Ahasuerus, both near and far, obliging them
to celebrate the fourteenth day of the month Adar,
and the fifteenth of the same month, annually, because on those days the Jews rid themselves of their
enemies, and it was a month which turned for them
from sorrow into gladness and from mourning into
a good day; that they should make them days of
feasting and rejoicing and sending portions to one
another and gifts to the poor (Esther 9:20–22).

The book of Esther includes descriptions of seven different feasts, which provide the basic structure of the book:

Ahasuerus's great banquet, 1:3ff
Ahasuerus's banquet for Esther, 2:18
Esther's first banquet, 5:5–8
Esther's second banquet, 7:1–10
Jews celebrate their reversal of fortune, 8:15–17
Jews celebrate their victory, 9:18
Mordecai institutes the permanent feast
    of Purim, 9:20–22

Not only does the theme of feasting recur throughout, but the feast scenes are turning points in the action of the story. The entire story began with the multiple feast in which Queen Vashti rebelliously refused to appear before the king (1:10–22). After Vashti was deposed, Ahasuerus searched for another queen, finally deciding upon Esther, whose selection was celebrated by a feast in her honor (2:18). Mordecai, like Vashti, refused to obey the king's orders (3:1–3), endangering all the Jews until Esther intervened to rescue her people by unfolding her counterplot against Haman in the two central feasts in the book. The remaining feasts were all celebrations in one way or another of Israel's victory against Haman the Agagite.

At the climax of the book is the institution of the permanent feast of Purim, and it has a multiple significance. Purim means "lots," and it is so named because the Lord controlled the lot that Haman threw, directing its decision for the benefit of Israel (3:7; 9:23–28). At Purim, Israel rejoiced in a God who controls the soaring eagle and the falling sparrow, the God of the lots who rules over all things for His church, who determines even those lots thrown in lands far to the east of His house in Jerusalem. Purim was also a feast of rest and Sabbath, the fourteenth and fifteenth days of the month Adar, which followed the day of victory and slaughter (9:16–17). Though Israel was overwhelmed by the sea of nations, the Lord spoke and she emerged as dry land. Purim thus was a victory celebration, an acknowledgment that Israel had been given rest from her enemies. Purim transformed Israel's mourning into gladness, her sackcloth into festal robes, her fast into feasting.

The Lord's Supper is our Purim. In it, we rejoice in the God of Pur whose predetermined will to save was worked out through the hands of wicked men (Acts 2:22–23). In it, we rest in the accomplished work of our Savior, who has delivered us from all enemies. In it, we acknowledge that at the consummation of the ages, history has moved from death to life, from mourning to gladness.

And the Supper is, like the feasts of Esther, a feast of wine. Wine flows freely through Esther. Her two feasts were "banquets of wine" (5:6; 7:8), and the wine was abundant at the initial feast of Ahasuerus (1:7–8). The emperor has often been scolded for this by well-meaning commentators, and Lemuel's warning against kings drinking wine is often brought into the discussion (Proverbs 31:2–9). In Esther, however, the wine has a different role. In the ancient world, the cup was often a symbol of power and rule. From the story of Joseph, we know that the cupbearer was a powerful and trusted official of the royal court with access to Pharaoh, and Nehemiah was also a cupbearer before the world emperor. Cups are fitting symbols of rule, particularly of the administration of justice: just as a host serves a portion of wine to each person, so a king allots to each what he deserves. Wine, further, is dangerous; it can be abused and make people do things they do not normally do; it can intoxicate and make people stumble aimlessly and drive recklessly. The king's justice, like the wine he apportions, can bring either delight or doom.

Rulers who are enthroned holding a chalice ultimately point to the Lord who, as the King of all the earth, also rules with a cup. In Jeremiah's prophecy against Edom, the Lord warned, "You will not be acquitted, but you will certainly drink" from Yahweh's cup (49:12). Often the Lord's cup is a cup of wrath, which He pours out upon the nations who rebel against Him. Having drunk the cup of the Lord, the nations reel to and fro, stumble and fall. Isaiah exhorted Jerusalem, "Rouse yourself! Rouse yourself! Arise,

O Jerusalem, you who have drunk from the Lord's hand the cup of His anger; the chalice of reeling you have drained to the dregs" (51:17, 22). In Jeremiah 25:15–17, the Lord gave Jeremiah the "cup of the wine of wrath" and told the prophet to "cause all the nations, to whom I send you, to drink it." As a result, "they shall drink and stagger and go mad because of the sword that I will send among them." Yahweh Himself ordered the nations, "Drink, be drunk, vomit, fall, and rise no more because of the sword which I will send among you" (Jeremiah 25:27–28).

Holding a cup, Ahasuerus passed judgment, causing rebels to fall. With his cup in his hand, he determined that Vashti "should come no more into the presence of King Ahasuerus" (Esther 1:19). With his cup in his hand, he gave the order concerning Haman: "Hang him on [the gallows]" (7:9). Ahasuerus poured out his wine; rebels drank, they reeled to and fro, they fell. But this same wine that brought destruction to Vashti and Haman filled the Jews with gladness, for the King had given them a favorable portion.

This theology of the cup underscores important dimensions of the Lord's Supper. If kings rule holding a chalice of wine, then each of us who sits at the Lord's table is being treated as a king, seated on thrones judging the twelve tribes of Israel. Since the cup we receive is the Lord's own cup, however, it can be either a cup of weal or of woe. We can rise from the table either gladdened or staggering. And we would all fall but for the fact that Jesus Himself has drunk His Father's cup to its dregs: "If possible, let this cup pass from Me." But it was not possible, and so He took our portion, staggered, and fell. He drained the cup that the King had given to us and now gives us to drink of His cup, a cup of joy.

20

Boisterous with Wine

> Yahweh of hosts will defend them. And they will devour, and trample on the sling stones; and they will drink, and be boisterous as with wine; and they will be filled like a basic, like the corners of the altar (Zechariah 9:15).

We have all seen the movie: the nerdy, longsuffering protagonist has endured torment at the hands of bigger and stronger villains until he can hardly stand it. But he has never been in a fight in his life and is too timid to stand up against his persecutors. Then . . . he takes his first slug of alcohol and turns into a fighting machine, punching out the school bully, rescuing the girl, riding the villains out of town on a rail. Even his hair begins to look better. In the movies at least, alcohol emboldens.

If any people needed emboldening, it was Israel during the early years after the return from Babylon. As Jeremiah had predicted decades before, Babylon had fallen and the Persians had taken over the empire. Early in his reign, Cyrus, the Persian conqueror, issued a decree permitting Jews to return to their land and begin rebuilding the temple. Several thousand exiles returned and quickly erected an altar in Jerusalem and celebrated the Feast of Booths (Ezra 3:4).

The people of the land, however, opposed the project and were able to enlist the help of the Persian government. For several years, the temple remained unfinished, but in the second year of Darius, two prophets appeared and urged the people to return to their work, the prophets Haggai and Zechariah. Under the preaching of these prophets, the dry bones of restoration Israel began to live; the Lord breathed into their nostrils and raised men from the dust.

In a series of visions that took place in the eleventh month of the second year of Darius (1:7), Zechariah received symbolic instruction concerning the temple. At the center of the series of visions, he saw the Lord cleansing the High Priest Joshua, reinstating him to priestly office, and a vision of two olive trees, representing Joshua and Zerubbabel, a priest and a king. These two were the "anointed ones, who are standing by the Lord of the whole earth" (4:14). The olive trees were supplying oil to a lampstand with seven lamps, and this was a sign that Joshua and Zerubbabel would provide the spiritual energy so that the lamp of Israel would not go out, so that Israel would shine like stars in the firmament. In both visions, the rebuilding of the temple was prominent: The first vision promises the coming of one called "Branch" (3:8), and later we learn that this Branch would build the house of God (6:12–13). Included in the vision of the olive trees was a promise of a restored temple: "The hands of Zerubbabel have laid the foundation of this house, and his hands will finish it" (4:9).

The temple project was at the center of Zechariah's visions, but rebuilding the temple was never an end in itself. At the beginning of the night of visions, Zechariah saw horses and horsemen standing in a myrtle grove (1:7–17) after patrolling the earth and finding it "peaceful and quiet" (1:10–11). Surprisingly, the angel of Yahweh did not take this as good news and cried out to Yahweh, "How long will you not have compassion for Jerusalem and the cities of Judah?" (1:12). Peace and quiet sound pleasant, but the angel of Yahweh knows that so long as the earth is so, Israel is still suffering the indignation of the Lord. Zechariah did not want the world to remain as it was, because the world as it was was in a sorry state. Instead, Zechariah wanted the Lord to shake the world until only those things that could not be shaken remained. At the end of the prophecy, Zechariah was told that his hopes would be realized. Another vision of horses closed the series, but this time the four horses, representing the four winds of heaven, were riding out to the ends of the earth, swifter than eagles to carry out the Lord's will (6:1–8). Now that the temple had been rebuilt, the Lord would shake the nations and bring in His kingdom. Rebuilding the temple was not an end in itself but a necessary part of the Lord's plan to gain a victory over rebellious nations and to extend His rule throughout the earth.

If Israel needed encouragement to finish building the temple, how much more did she need reassurance during the global earthquake that, according to Zechariah's visions, was to follow. In the latter part of Zechariah's prophecy, he delivered two oracles concerning the shaking of the nations and the effects it would have on Israel. Zechariah described Yahweh's triumphant progression from Hamath toward Philistia. Despite their preparations and defenses, even Tyre and Sidon would not stand before Him, and Yahweh would "cut off the pride of the Philistines" (9:1–8). Because Yahweh was dealing with her enemies, Jerusalem would rejoice at His coming. Like another Solomon, Israel's King would extend the kingdom "from sea to sea, and from the

River to the ends of the earth" (9:9–10; see Psalm 72:8).

It is difficult to know when this prophecy was fulfilled. Verses 9–10 are quoted in Matthew 21 and applied to Jesus' triumphal entry into Jerusalem, but the whole passage is also reminiscent of Alexander's conquest of the Middle East. At least from verse eleven on, Zechariah was looking ahead to events in the "intertestamental period," when faithful Jews battled to turn back the infiltration of Greek culture and thought into Israel. Yahweh of hosts promised to stir up the sons of Zion against the sons of "Javan" (9:13), and Javan was the biblical name for Greece (related to "Ionia"). Yahweh would use Judah as His bow and Ephraim as His arrows (9:13), making His people weapons in His warfare against Greece. He would flash His arrows from above like lightning, scattering His enemies before Him. And the Lord would be victorious: He "will save them in that day, as the flock of His people" (9:16).

In this context of warfare and triumph, food and drink play an important role. Yahweh's people, His weapons, would "devour" their enemies, drink wine, and become boisterous—as filled with wine as the basin at the foot of the altar was filled with blood, filled with wine like the blood-caked "corners of the altar" (9:15). What Israel would find exhilarating was partly the "wine-blood" of her enemies, who had been slaughtered before her. But the passage pictures Israel drunk with another kind of wine: filled with the wine of Yahweh's Spirit, Israel would be bold, wild, untamed, boisterous in battle. This suggests one dimension of the symbolism of wine in the Lord's Supper: it loosens our inhibitions so that we will fight the Lord's battles in a kind of drunken frenzy. If this sounds impious, how much more Psalm 78:65, where the Divine Warrior Himself is described as a mighty man overcome with wine?   Yahweh fights like Samson, but far more ferociously than Samson: He fights like a drunken Samson! Grape juice, it must be said, simply does not carry the same punch. Deprived of wine at the Lord's table, it is no wonder that we fight our battles so timidly, no wonder we stay so nerdy and are constantly plagued by bullies.

Wine emboldens the soldier for battle, and wine also flows at the victory celebration that follows. Those who devoured their enemies would devour a victory feast. This is the feast that we enjoy: the Lord has aimed His arrows not only at Greece but at all our enemies, at the greatest enemies—sin and death—and has driven them from the field. He makes us boisterous with wine, and He makes us flourish with grain and new wine.

21

Contempt for Yahweh's Altar

> You are presenting defiled food upon My altar. But you say, 'How have we defiled thee?' in that you say, 'The table of the Lord is to be despised' (Malachi 1:7).

Some Protestants object when high church traditions claim that the Lord's Supper is celebrated at an "altar." Fearing that this implies that the Supper is a new sacrifice of Christ, and fearing that this idea undermines the New Testament's emphasis on the once-for-all character of Christ's death, Protestants insist, "It's not an altar; it's a table." Such fears, it must be said, are quite real. Some forms of Eucharistic doctrine do at least raise doubts about the completed character of the atonement, and these doctrines should be opposed. But it does not follow that "altar" is an inappropriate term for the Lord's Table. The reason for this is obvious from Malachi 1: in Scripture, the altar *is* a table, one from which both God and man eat. According to Leviticus 21:21–23, the altar was the table on which the Lord's "bread" is offered, but under the Law, priests and sometimes lay Israelites were also permitted to eat from the Lord's table. Since they were Yahweh's servants, priests in particular were allowed to eat from the abundance of their Master's storehouse.

Malachi, writing during the postexilic period, targeted these priests for special rebuke because they were mistreating the Lord's table. His prophecy began with a dialogue between Yahweh and Israel that reminded Israel of her origins in her father Jacob. Jacob, Yahweh said, I have loved, but Esau I have hated, and the Lord went on to describe the devastation of Edom, the people of Esau (1:2–4). At first blush, this sounds encouraging for Israel: "We are," they might have concluded, "the objects of God's love, not like those hateful descendants of Esau." But the exchange makes clear that God's love is an electing love, a love that chooses certain people and rejects others. Should she turn from her Lord, Israel might also be "beaten down" until she was called the "wicked territory, and the people toward whom the Lord is indignant forever" (1:4). This was certainly the way that Paul understood the passage, which he quotes in Romans 9. For Paul, "Esau" was not somebody outside Israel but hated ones within the covenant people.

The danger that Israel might end up like Edom was a real one, as Malachi went on to explain in detail. From 1:6 through the end of chapter three, Malachi did little but list the sins of the restoration people: priests had "caused many to stumble by the instruction" (2:8). Judah had profaned the Lord's sanctuary by marrying "the daughter of a foreign god" (2:11), and divorce from the daughters of the true God was rampant (2:14–16). Israel had robbed Yahweh by refusing to bring the full tithe into His storehouse (3:7–12). For these reasons, the Lord threatened to come "burning like a furnace" to consume the chaff and all the dead branches of the vine of Israel (4:1–3). Israel could not rest in the fact that Yahweh loved Jacob. She must remember that Yahweh hated Esau, and fear.

Malachi's first charge against the priests was that they

despised Yahweh. Priests were servants of the Lord's house, adopted as His sons, and yet they had not given Him the honor He was due as the Father and Master of His house (1:6). Getting down to specifics, the prophet claimed that the priests despised the Lord by despising His table, His altar, in several ways. All sacrificial animals had to be unblemished, and the Law specifically prohibited animals that were "blind or fractured or maimed or having a running sore or eczema or scabs" from being offered on His table (Leviticus 22:22). But the priests of Malachi's day had violated this commandment, offering the "blind for sacrifice," sacrificing animals who were "lame and sick," even bringing animals taken by "robbery" (Malachi 1:8, 13–14). Animals that priests would not think of offering to the Persian provincial governor were being brought to Yahweh's table (1:8). Yahweh would rather shut down the temple, put out the fire on His altar, and move east than to accept such offerings from the priests (1:10). Like Hophni and Phinehas, the sons of Eli, these priests despised the offering of the Lord (1 Samuel 2:17), and the Lord was threatening to turn their light into darkness.

Priests despised the table of the Lord in another way as well: they said that its "fruit, its food is to be despised," and they did "disdainfully sniff at it." According to the Law, priests received portions of the sacrificial food for their own consumption. In many cases, these portions were very generous; the priest who offered a peace offering received the thigh, a sizable chunk of flesh, for himself. Yet, the priests of the restoration did not receive it thankfully, disdaining it as if to say, "It's not so much food, nor so good either."

We are no longer required to keep the rules that the priests were ignoring, but Malachi's charges are very relevant to our attitudes toward the Lord's table. Priests of Malachi's day were rebuked for failing to observe the details of the sacrificial rituals, and the God we worship is still the God of details and is still indignant when we reject His commandments for the sake of our traditions. One example will have to do here: it is abundantly clear that Jesus instituted a meal that involved wine, not unfermented grape juice, and at several points in this book, we have examined some reasons for His choice of wine. Yet, in our great wisdom, we have decided that wine is so dangerous that it has no place in the house of the Lord on the Sabbath day, all the while ignoring the fact that the *danger* of wine is precisely one of the reasons for drinking it.

More generally, contempt for the Lord's table is contempt for the Lord of the table, and this is as true for the church as it was for ancient Israel. Matthew Henry wisely applied these verses of Malachi to "those who live in a careless neglect of holy ordinances." If this is the case, many churches today live in open contempt of their Lord. The Lord has provided a generous meal for His people; we have a sacrifice from which even those who served in the temple had no right to eat. Yet we complain that it makes the service too long and it is inconvenient and it is repetitive and it is boring and maybe the roast in the oven will burn. "My, how tiresome it is," we sniff (Malachi 1:13), and thereby prove ourselves sons of Esau.

22

Table Manners of the Kingdom

And he began speaking a parable to the invited guests when He noticed how they had been picking out the places of honor (Luke 14:7).

Table manners distinguish man from the beasts. The robin outside my window is tugging and tugging at a determined worm, and as soon as he pulls it loose, he unceremoniously swallows it down whole. If one of my children ate spaghetti in the same way, he would get a stern look, at least.

Table manners distinguish man from the beasts because they mark man as a cultural being as well as creature of nature. Indeed, table manners are among first cultural habits we acquire. Toddlers move from the high chair to the table when they are able to eat without smearing tomato sauce in their hair or tossing leftovers on the floor. When their behavior becomes "civilized," they are admitted to the table of the small *cives*, the small city that is the family, and as they become increasingly adept at polite behavior, they are admitted to a wider *polis*. Learning table manners is a part of being initiated into a particular civilization, and as manners are acquired, the person begins to take on the character of an Arab or a Zulu or a Pole. Though table manners are in many respects quite similar across many cultures, the differences are significant enough to identify a person as a member of a particular group. In *The Rituals of Dinner*, Margaret Visser points out that in some cultures, fasting is necessary before a feast, and "exclaiming with pleasure, smacking one's lips, and so on might be thought both polite and benevolent," but "other cultures prefer to stress that food is not everything, and guzzling is disgusting."

Entering God's kingdom means acquiring a new set of habits, and in Jesus' teaching this new manner of life is sometimes described as a new set of table manners. Meals, after all, were at the heart of Jesus' ministry, both in His teaching and His actions. The message of Jesus' preaching was the imminent coming of the kingdom of God. When He preached on this theme, He was referring to the fulfillment of God's promises to restore Israel, and, through Israel, the world. God's kingdom was the answer to the sin of Adam, the sin of Cain, the sin at the tower of Babel, the sin of Israel. All effects of sin were to be reversed, whether personal or political, in the soul or in society. Jesus was telling everyone that in His ministry this was beginning to appear, as the God who called light out of darkness began to call a new creation into being.

Oddly, at least to us, Jesus' most frequent image of this restored and perfected world was the imagery of feasting. Jesus marveled at the centurion's faith, which was greater than any He had discovered in Israel, and He observed that "many will come from the east and west and recline with Abraham, Isaac, and Jacob in the kingdom of heaven" (Matthew 8:5–13). Conversion of the Gentiles was part of Israel's hope, and, according to Jesus, this hope, like all the others, was now coming to pass. Jesus told parables that depicted the kingdom as a wedding feast to which people are invited from east and west, gathered in from the highways and byways (Matthew 22:1–14; Luke 14:16–24; see John 2:1–11).

In these parables and sayings, Jesus was not merely expressing a hope that someday, off in the distant future, God would fulfill His promises. On the contrary, Jesus understood His own ministry as the beginning of that fulfillment. When His disciples asked Jesus why He did not make them fast, Jesus answered that fasting was inappropriate for the time: "The sons of the bridal chamber cannot mourn as long as the bridegroom is with them" (9:15). Jesus, the Bridegroom of Israel, had come to win His bride, and that meant that the wedding feast had begun. Elsewhere, Jesus contrasted His ministry with that of John using the same contrast of fasting and feasting. John came fasting, calling the people to prepare themselves for the Lord's arrival. Jesus was the Lord Himself, who came "eating and drinking" with such gusto that He was accused of being a glutton and a drunkard (Matthew 11:16–19).

For Jesus, then, "feast" was not just a "metaphor" for the kingdom. As Jesus announced the feast of the kingdom, He also brought it into reality through His own feasting. Unlike many theologians, He did not come preaching an ideology, promoting ideas, or teaching moral maxims. He came teaching about the feast of the kingdom, *and* He came feasting in the kingdom. Jesus did not go around merely talking about eating and drinking; he went around eating and drinking. A lot. As we read the gospels, especially Luke, the basis for the Jewish charge that Jesus was a glutton and drunkard takes on some plausibility. It seems that every other chapter of Luke's gospel shows Jesus at a meal. Levi gave a banquet for Jesus at his house, where Jesus talked about the difference between John's ministry of fasting and

His own work (5:29–39). Turn the page, and we see Jesus and His disciples eating on the Sabbath (6:1–5). One of the Pharisees asked Jesus to dine with him and while there a woman anointed Him (7:36–50). Then Jesus fed five thousand with five loaves and two fishes (9:10–17) and moved on to have dinner with Mary and Martha (10:38–42). Another Sabbath, another feast, again at the house of a Pharisee (14:1–24), and when He arrived in Jerusalem, he sent His disciples to make preparations for His final meal with them (22:7–30). So prominent is this theme in Luke that one recent commentary is entitled *Lord of the Banquet*.

As "Lord of the banquet," Jesus set the protocols for participation. Burning issues of etiquette like belching and picking teeth were outside His concern, but He used the feast to represent the demands of discipleship. Luke 14 describes Jesus' meal at the home of an unnamed Pharisee and shows how much instruction Jesus could derive from the festive metaphor. This meal took place on a Sabbath, and during the meal, Jesus healed a man suffering from dropsy. Though the Pharisees expressed their disapproval through their sullen silence, Jesus in fact did nothing at all contrary to the Law. He was instead showing the true nature of the Sabbath, as a time of celebration, resurrection, and healing (14:1–6). He was showing that, in His kingdom at least, the Sabbath is a day for feasting.

Observing the scramble for places of honor at the meal, Jesus commented on the radically different precepts that govern His table: "When you are invited, go and recline in the last place" because "everyone who exalts himself shall be humbled, and he who humbles himself shall be exalted" (14:10–11). Jesus showed that, at His table in the kingdom, humility is the way to honor.

Noting the guest list, Jesus pointed out how

hospitality can arise from ambition as much as from generosity; throwing a big bash can be more about getting than giving. A host shapes his guest list in the hope that those who are invited will "invite you in return, and repayment come to you." Calculations of this sort have no place at Jesus' table: His disciples should invite the "poor, the crippled, the lame, the blind," those who can repay nothing. In this way, they show themselves to be sons of their heavenly Father, whose guest list is likewise full of those who cannot return the favor (14:12–14).

The Supper of the church is not a different meal from the meals that Jesus celebrated with his disciples during His ministry. What we enjoy is still the feast of the kingdom, with Jesus among us as our host and food, and the same table conduct that Jesus prescribed for His disciples applies to us, both at the table and elsewhere. What we do at the table manifests the kind of people we are or, at least, aspire to be. At this table, we show that we are a joyful people, celebrating God's Sabbath gift of rest and healing. At this table, it is not the self-promoting but the humble who are called to the higher seats. To this table, we welcome all sorts and conditions of men. Life in the kingdom, in short, still demands that we adopt a new set of table manners, and as we observe this etiquette, we become increasingly civilized according to the codes of the city of God.

23
The Joy of the Father

We had to be merry and rejoice, for this brother of yours was dead and has begun to live, and was lost and has been found (Luke 15:32).

Casting a Biblical epic must be a nightmare, because Scripture rarely provides physical descriptions of characters. We have no way of knowing whether Adam was tall or short, whether Eve was blonde or brunette, whether Cain was swarthy and Abel fair or the opposite, whether Abraham had that long white beard you see in Bible cartoons, or whether Moses looked more like Charlton Heston or Danny DeVito. Even when Scripture gives a physical description, it is never sufficiently detailed for a portrait. Women are described as "beautiful," but we are left in the dark about the color of their hair or eyes. We know that Saul was "a choice and handsome man" who "from his shoulders and up was taller than any of the people" (1 Samuel 9:2), but there are all sorts of species in the genus, "tall handsome king." David was "ruddy, with beautiful eyes and a handsome appearance" (1 Samuel 16:12), and we know he later wore a beard because he let his saliva dribble into it to escape Achish of Gath (1 Samuel 21:13). That is about as complete a physical description as you can find in the Bible.

In a sense, this reticence about physical appearance should not surprise us. The Bible is not a novel, and its writers are not interested, as novelists usually are, in creating a feeling of "authenticity." Rather, Scripture is revelation of the history of salvation, and the descriptions that are included contribute to the theological point of a story. Esau was described as a hairy hunter because he was a predatory beast, ruled by his belly (Genesis 25:25), and the ruddiness of his skin is immediately associated with his desire for "red stuff, red stuff" (Genesis 25:30). When the Israelites saw that Saul stretched up toward the firmament, they concluded that he would make a great warrior-king. Ironically, when the Philistine giant Goliath appeared on the scene, the Israelite giant stayed in his tent, quaking with fear. David is described in terms that recall Joseph—fittingly, because like Joseph he endured much suffering before inheriting the kingdom.

Of all the people that Jesus encountered in His years of ministry, the gospels give physical descriptions of only a few, and of these the most famous is Zaccheus, described by Luke as "small in stature" (Luke 19:3). Of course, this is important to the story because it explains why a grown man was climbing a tree as Jesus passed by. But the significance of Zaccheus's size goes further, for his physical size symbolizes his reputation among his neighbors. Being a tax collector, he was, in the eyes of the people of Jericho, a "small" man in every sense. That is why the crowd began to grumble when Jesus invited Himself to Zaccheus's house: "He has gone to be the guest of a man who is a sinner" (Luke 19:7). How dare Jesus visit the home of such a "small" man! In response to this criticism, Jesus gave what I. Howard Marshall has called the theme sentence of the entire gospel: "The Son of Man has come to seek and to save that which was lost" (Luke 19:6). Luke is the gospel of the seeking God, and the ones God seeks are often those who are small in the eyes of the world.

Throughout his gospel, Luke highlighted Jesus' encounters with and compassion toward the outcasts, the "small" ones, of Jewish society. Luke was the only evangelist to record the Magnificat, reminiscent of the song of Hannah (1 Samuel 2), with its stirring praise to the Mighty One who scatters the proud and exalts the humble, who fills the hungry and sends the rich away empty (Luke 1:46–55). Luke alone recorded Jesus' sermon at Nazareth, where Jesus announced the coming of the favorable year when good news would be proclaimed to the poor and downtrodden (Luke 4:16–21). Luke alone recorded the parables of the prodigal, the publican and Pharisee, and the good Samaritan. Jesus not only came seeking but seeking especially those whom everyone else had stopped seeking. Big people do not need to be sought, because everyone sees them and they have a knack for keeping themselves visible. Finding those who are "small in stature," however, requires diligence.

Seeking and finding the lost is closely entwined, in Luke's gospel, with feasting. Jesus sought out small people for the specific purpose of inviting them to share a table with Him. Around His table gathered the dregs that Jesus formed into His new community. The feast, further, displayed the character of the salvation that the lost would receive, the new shape that Israel was assuming in Jesus' ministry. The Israel of Jesus was not to be a spiritual elite. It was an Israel constituted of the humble and contrite, an Israel of repentant publicans and harlots, an Israel that included many from east and west.

Jesus' focus on the "small" was a direct rebuke to first-century Jews, especially the Pharisees whose program for

the renewal of Israel was a program of separation. By trans-
forming Israel into a holy, separated people, the Pharisees
hoped to hasten Israel's restoration. For the Pharisees,
maintaining cleanness at meals was of central importance;
to maintain their holiness, Israel had to keep away from
defiling foods, from defiling table fellows, and from food
that had not been tithed. Only if they maintained these
rigid boundaries of cleanliness and holiness would Israel's
hopes be realized. Then came Jesus, flagrantly and consciously
snubbing every one of their taboos and gaining widespread
support among the people in the process. From the Pharisees' perspective, if Jesus succeeded, He would doom Israel
to defilement and to perpetual cursing. No wonder they
concluded that one man had to die for the sake of the people.

Three parables in Luke 15 bring these themes to a focus; they have essentially the same plot: someone loses a
thing of value (though perhaps valueless to others), searches
diligently, and rejoices when it is found. At the conclusion
of the parable of the lost sheep, Jesus made His point ex-
plicit: "I tell you that in the same way, there will be more
joy in heaven over one sinner who repents, than over ninety-
nine righteous persons who need no repentance" (v. 7).
Jesus also summarized the meaning of the second parable
in slightly, though significantly, different words: "In the
same way, I tell you, there is joy in the presence of the angels of God over one sinner who repents" (v. 10). "Joy in
the presence of the angels" is *God's* joy in the presence of
the angels. Like a mighty warrior, He "exults with joy" over
His restored Bride and "rejoices over [her] with shouts of
joy" (Zephaniah 3:17). When a sheep returns, the Good
Shepherd celebrates.

Jesus told these parables because the Pharisees were com-
plaining that Jesus was too free with His table: He

"receives sinners and eats with them" (v. 2). Each of the parables was a defense of His practice of eating and drinking with sinners. In the first two parables, Jesus was saying that His feasts manifested the joy of the God who seeks and finds. To the joyless Pharisees, Jesus said, "Of course, I am eating and drinking and celebrating with the smallest of the small, with sinners. What better thing to do when something that had been lost is finally found?"

The third of the parables, the one we know as the parable of the "prodigal son," has the same focus. Like the shepherd and the woman of the previous parables, the father loses something he dearly loves, and his eagerness to meet his son on the road shows that he has been waiting and watching diligently for what he lost (v. 20). Having found his son, he rejoices, and to express his joy, the father calls his servants to butcher the fatted calf and prepare a great feast. Feasting is the concrete expression of the father's joy at the recovery of his lost son, at the resurrection of his "dead" son (v. 32; cf. vv. 6, 9), and the feasts of Jesus also express the overflowing joy of a Father. To enter into the feast involves not only receiving the joy that the Father gives; it also means sharing in the Father's own joy over every prodigal who has come to his senses in a distant land.

Jesus' parable was at the same time a sharp rebuke to the Pharisees, and their angry reaction to Jesus becomes more understandable when we recognize, as N. T. Wright has pointed out, that Jesus' parable is an allegory of the history of Israel: a son leaves His father, as Israel had turned from Yahweh. He goes to a foreign land, as Israel had gone into exile. Having come to his senses, he returns, and his father greets him joyously. The Pharisees would have recognized this story as Israel's own story, which, they believed, would come to a climax with a feast of return. But Jesus turned the story upside down by making the despised "sinners" the heroes of the story. They were the ones who were truly returning from exile; they were God's true "son," which is to say, the true Israel; they were the small ones over whom the Father was rejoicing. And they were all these things precisely because they came to Jesus and shared His table.

Oh, Jesus put the Pharisees in the story too. They had complained about Jesus feasting with sinners, and Jesus responded by telling a story about an older brother who grumbled when his father threw a feast for a sinner! The Pharisees were cast in the role of villain, the elder brother who cuts himself off from his father's joy by isolating himself from the feast of his father's joy. They were the sons of the kingdom, peering through the windows from outside the banquet hall, gnashing their teeth at the publicans and prostitutes who were eating and drinking with Jesus in His Father's kingdom.

24
Blessed City,
Heavenly Salem

And when he had gone back up, and had broken the
bread and tasted, he talked with them a long while,
until daybreak, and so departed (Acts 20:11).

Early Christians adopted the word *ekklesia* ("church") from
the Septuagint, the Greek translation of the Old Testament, which used *ekklesia* to describe the "assembly" of Israel (see Deuteronomy 9:10). When Christians used this
term, they were claiming to be the true Israel, the true assembly of Yahweh. But the word was also used in secular
Greek, and in that context, it was a political term, referring to the "assembly" of (male) citizens of a Greek city-
state or *polis*. Aristotle used the term, for example, when he
located the sovereign power of the *polis* in the "assembly."
In using this political term, the early Christians were saying something about their community. It implied that the
church was not a private club nor an association for people
who shared an interest in religious things. Rather, the church
was an *ekklesia*, the sovereign assembly of a new *polis*.

Only one passage of the New Testament uses the word
ekklesia in this secular Greek sense, and that is in Luke's
account of Paul's activities in Ephesus in Acts 19. Paul's

ministry met with considerable success in Ephesus, a significant city on the western coast of Asia Minor, and many responded to Paul by turning from their idolatry and magical practices to the living God (19:18–20). Annoyed at Paul's preaching, an Ephesian named Demetrius gathered the guild of silversmiths together and whipped them into a fury with his incendiary attacks on the apostle: "Not only is there danger that this trade of ours fall into disrepute, but also that the temple of the great goddess Artemis be regarded as worthless and that she whom all of Asia and the world worship should even be dethroned from her magnificence" (19:27). Shouting about the greatness of Artemis of the Ephesians, the people rushed into the theater, dragging Paul's companions with them. Luke calls this mob an *"ekklesia"* (v. 32). This was hardly a normal meeting of the Ephesian assembly: the whole city was in confusion; the artisans were dragging Paul's companions into the theater; everyone was shouting something different, so that once they had gathered in the assembly, no one was sure why they were there. Finally the town clerk had to break up the mob, after they had been shouting praise to Artemis of the Ephesians for two hours. This is hardly the sober, deliberative body celebrated by political theorists from Aristotle to this day. Even the town clerk recognized that this was not a "regular assembly" (*ekklesia*, v. 39).

In the entire New Testament, this is the only picture of a Greek city-state and its vaunted democratic system at work. To be sure, Luke did include somewhat more sympathetic Greeks, the inquisitive philosophers of Mars Hill, who rejected Paul's gospel but at least did not start a riot in the process (Acts 17). Of the Greek *polis* and its *ekklesia*, however, Luke gave nothing but this deeply ironic picture. This riotous Ephesian gathering, Luke was saying, was the

kind of assembly one found in Greece; it was the best the
Greek world had to offer. The city-state, with its assembly, was not the birthplace of freedom and democracy but
a place of violence, chaos, and confusion. For Luke, the
character of Greek civilization was revealed by the character of its *ekklesia*.

This becomes even more profoundly interesting when
we look at a similar incident several chapters over, where
there is another riot, another city thrown into confusion,
another "assembly" (Acts 21:27–22:29). The parallels between the two incidents are striking: in both, some men
roused others to fury (19:25f; 21:27f.); in both, Paul
was accused of preaching against basic religious institutions and symbols; in both, the whole city was aroused into
confusion (19:29; 21:30); in both, the mob rushed hither
and yon, dragging the apostle and his friends with them
(19:29; 21:30); in both, the people gathered and shouted
so much that no one could tell what the others were saying
(19:32; 21:34); in both, someone tried to speak and was
shouted down (19:34; 22:22–23). The incidents themselves were similar, and Luke wrote his accounts in such a
way as to highlight the similarities.

The second riot did not, however, occur in a Greek
city-state but in Jerusalem, the city of Yahweh. Here the
people were not pagan Greeks but Jews, not worshipers of
Artemis but the upholders of the laws and institutions of
Abraham, Moses and David. By calling attention to the similarities between the two incidents, Luke revealed the com-
monality of the Greek and Jewish *ekklesiai*, the similarity
between the life of the Greek community and that of the
Jewish community. Confronted with the gospel, both responded with confusion and violence.

In 1 Corinthians 15:32, Paul wrote of fighting with

wild beasts at Ephesus. While some commentators have interpreted the reference to wild beasts literally, suggesting that Paul was placed in the arena, I think that this is an allusion to the incident recorded in Acts 19. The wild beasts were the Ephesians themselves; they were the strong bulls from Bashan in Psalm 22, the lions that attack and tear the Psalmist in Psalms 57; 35:17; 58:6. To Paul, the Greek *ekklesia* was a bestial assembly, full of people rushing, dragging, roaring—all actions of predators attacking their prey. Luke was showing the effects of worshiping the forces of nature, whether birds or fish, whether the earth itself or the fertility goddess Artemis. In the assembly, confronted with the gospel, the bestial reality of this civilization was revealed. But, if the Ephesians were wild beasts, the Jews were equally so, for they too beat, tore, and dragged their prey when there was none to deliver.

In these two incidents Luke pronounced his (and the Lord's) verdict on the ancient ways of ordering human life, on the cultures of the old creation. In the assembly, and in response to the gospel, it became clear that the future hopes of the world for peace could not lie either in the sea of nations or in the land of Israel. An order of justice would not arise from either of the ancient *ekklesiai*, whether the Greek assembly or the Jewish gathering in Jerusalem. Neither Greek democracy nor Jewish theocracy could bring in the new world promised by the prophets. Jew and Greek are alike Adamic civilizations. Being under the curse of death, they can produce nothing living. Both are in bondage to the "elementary principles of this world" (Galatians 4:3, 9). Jew and Greek alike had succumbed to the beast, the serpent, and acted like their father, who was a murderer from the beginning. Jerusalem and Athens had become bestial civilizations, and both stood in need of a beast-master, a

Man capable of taming them.

Between these two incidents, and throughout the book of Acts, Luke told of an alternative *ekklesia*, a different assembly that manifested a different "way" of life in another kind of city. As in Ephesus and Jerusalem, the character of this society was revealed in the conduct of its citizens when they gathered together (20:7–12). This assembly came together on the first day, the beginning of a new week, the day of a new creation. They gathered not with shouting and confusion but in praise to *listen* to the word preached. They gathered to break bread not to break heads. To break bread is to share it, to distribute it from hand to hand, to form a circle of bread-eaters, a community that is one body because all share in one and the same loaf. In this new *ekklesia*, there were no beasts dragging and tearing. Here the serpent did not rule but the Man, Jesus. Its assembly was a passage, a Passover, a *transitus* that moved its participants from death to new life, signified when (at midnight!) Eutychus was raised to life and received at the feast.

It must be stressed that this new *ekklesia* did not achieve its peaceable state by ignoring or barricading itself from the bestial assemblies that it confronted. As Michael Welker has recently emphasized, the meal that the church celebrates was instituted on the "night in which He was betrayed," and it memorializes the crucified Jesus, who was delivered up to death by Jews and Gentiles alike. Paul was not the first to be beaten, torn, and dragged by wild beasts. In celebrating the Supper as the city of peace, we are not encouraging optimism about the world, hoping naively that things will improve if people will just play nicely. If the church learns anything from its gospel, she should learn that people do not play nicely. This meal instead announces that the old city died in killing the Prince of Life and that a new city has been formed in His resurrection.

"Breaking bread" is thus not only a sign of the communion that the members of Christ have with one another. It is a sign that a new society has been created, and it is an effective sign, bringing to reality what it symbolizes, forming that new society around the table of the Lord. Gathering at the Lord's table forms the *ekklesia* at the center of a new and better city.

25

Flee Idolatry

> You cannot drink the cup of the Lord and the cup of demons; you cannot partake of the table of the Lord and the table of demons (1 Corinthians 10:21).

Factionalism is as old as the church herself, nowhere better exemplified than in Paul's letters to the Corinthians. Quarrels, strife, and division characterized this church, as each member proudly wore the teeshirt of his favorite apostle. Paul's response was to emphasize the unity of Christ. To divide the church into factions divides "Christ," since He is inseparable from His body. "Has Christ been divided?" Paul asked incredulously after listing the various factions of the congregation (1:13; cf. 12:12–13). So close is Christ identified with His church that rending the latter is equivalent to tearing Christ in pieces.

1 Corinthians is also the New Testament book that gives the most extensive coverage to baptism and the Lord's Supper, and Paul brought both into play in his polemics against Corinthian factionalism, since both are signs of the unity of the body. No one, Paul said, was baptized into his name, or into the name of Peter or Apollos. Rather, all had been baptized into the name of Christ, and since all had

been baptized to become His disciples, they should not be acting as if they were disciples of men (1:13–16). Later, in 12:13, Paul again brought up baptism to emphasize the unity of the church, especially the unity of Jews and Gentiles in the "one new Man" that is the body of Christ. Since baptism is a sign of the unity, discord among the baptized muddies the waters. Sporting the Pauline teeshirt is an offense against baptism, in which we were clothed with Christ.

Likewise, Paul treated the Lord's Supper as a sign of the unity of the one Christ: "Since there is one loaf, we who are many are one body; for we all partake of the one loaf" (10:16). Paul struck the same chord in the great Eucharistic passage in 11:17–34. He condemned the Corinthians because there were "divisions" in the body when they came together (v. 19); they did not show deference for one another but rather "each one takes his own supper first" (v. 21). These divisions had so completely undermined the meaning of the Supper that, whatever their intentions, the Corinthians were not actually eating the Lord's Supper at all (v. 20). They were grumbling at Thanksgiving, burning the flag on the Fourth of July.

"Has Christ been divided?" The answer is, in a sense, "Yes," for at the table the bread is broken and distributed to the church, just as at the cross His body was torn for us. But this division of Christ has the goal of uniting the church. On the cross, Christ was broken in the process of breaking down the dividing wall separating Jew and Gentile; in the Supper, Christ is divided so that His one loaf can feed many.

Not only was the Corinthian church rent internally by factionalism, but it was also corrupted by influences from the world. Elsewhere, Paul had written that strife and quarrels are fruits of the flesh (Galatians 5), and so Paul's attack on Corinthian schism included an exhortation to separate from the ways of the world. The Supper is also brought up in this connection, especially in chapters 10–11, which are part of a larger discussion of meat sacrificed to idols that begins in chapter eight. Concerns about eating meat sacrificed to idols are obscure to us, but in a city like Corinth, much of the meat offered at the butcher's shop had been sacrificed to idols. Indeed, in ancient Greek, the same word was used for both "butcher" and "sacrificer," and procedures for butchery were normally religiously prescribed. As with Israel in the wilderness (Leviticus 17), all Greek butchery was sacrifice. If Christians were forbidden to eat meat sacrificed to idols, they would have to follow the Pythagorean example and become vegetarians.

But Paul did not urge Christians to become vegetarians, much less Pythagoreans. Rather, he said there was no sin in eating meat sacrificed to idols. Idols are nothing, since, as every Jew knew, there is only one God. So long as food was received with thanksgiving, it should be received without any qualms of conscience, as a gift from the hand of the One who opens His hand to satisfy the desires of every living thing (8:1–5). Paul reiterated this principle in chapter ten: "Eat anything that is sold in the meat market, without asking questions for conscience' sake; for the earth is the Lord's, and all it contains. If one of the unbelievers invites you, and you wish to go, eat anything that is set before you, without asking questions for conscience' sake" (vv. 25–27). Freedom to eat meat sacrificed to idols, however, was limited by the demands of love: "Take care lest this liberty of yours somehow become a stumbling block to the weak," lest your eating offend any brothers for whom Christ died (8:10–12).

When we get to 1 Corinthians 10:14–22, however,

Paul's argument appears to shift ground and prohibit eating meat sacrificed to idols. Gentiles sacrificed to demons and became communicants with demons in the process, and Paul warned the Corinthians not "to become sharers in demons" (10:21). The resolution to this apparent contradiction is to notice that Paul was addressing two different sets of circumstances. On the one hand, all meat available at the local butcher's was to be accepted gratefully. On the other hand, Paul prohibited Christians from actually participating in the sacrificial rituals of pagan worship. On the one hand, it is possible to receive meat sacrificed to idols and give thanks to God. On the other hand, it is not possible to eat a meal dedicated to Luna the moon goddess and simultaneously give thanks to God.

Though he did not bring them out explicitly, Paul's instructions here had far-reaching political implications. He was not merely exhorting the Corinthians to separate from pagan "religion," but to separate from the pagan social and political system. Unlike cities of the modern West, the Greco-Roman city was as much a religious as it was a political organization, where citizens were expected to participate in civic festivals. Ancient civic feasts were not like our national holidays, "secular" holidays celebrating our founding. Rather, they were thoroughly religious feasts, including sacrifices to the gods of the city, whether Athena in Athens, or Artemis in Ephesus. Refusal to participate in the feasts of idols was a refusal of one privilege of citizenship. Paul did not require that Christians renounce all rights as citizens, and he himself made use of his rights as a Roman. But the fact that the Corinthians ate at the Lord's table meant that they were citizens of another city, the heavenly Jerusalem, and their citizenship in Corinth had to be radically subordinate to that.

For us as well, eating and drinking at the Lord's table makes a political statement. If we share the Lord's table, we cannot be Americans first, or even first of all members of our families. Far above all, we are to be identified as members of the body of Christ, sharers in His table. Citizenship in America or in a city, or membership in a family are goods *only if* such groups contribute to our life in the body of Christ. When a nation or a city or a family is organized in opposition to Him, we must refuse the invitation to sit at their tables. With abortion rights, homosexual marriages, and other evils now defended as basic American freedoms, perhaps American Christians will someday conclude that celebrating the Fourth of July is the moral equivalent of feasting at a table of demons, incompatible with feasting at Christ's table. We are nowhere close to that point, but unless we are willing to contemplate the possibility, we have not grasped the radical demands of the Lord's table. Proper participation in the Supper reinforces one dimension of the church's calling and mission, which includes, as Rowan Williams has powerfully suggested, the "fundamental Christian vocation of *not* belonging."

26
Justification and
Table Fellowship

Prior to the coming of certain men from James,
[Peter] used to eat with the Gentiles; but when
they came, he began to withdraw and hold himself
aloof, fearing the party of the circumcision (Galatians 2:12).

Galatians is a very difficult letter, partly because Paul was
dealing with profound theological issues but even more
because Paul was very upset when he wrote it. It shows.
Arguments begin, only to fade opaquely in the middle, long
before we have gotten the drift of Paul's thought. Every
sentence, it seems, trails off in a lingering ellipse. Since the
Bible is God's Word, Galatians says exactly what God intended it to say. But it is evident that in this book God
intended to send an emotionally charged message to His
church.

Paul was upset because he discerned that the gospel
was at stake, and Paul hammered on this point by using the
noun "gospel" and the verb form, "preach the gospel," twelve
times in the first two chapters alone. Apparently, the Galatians, or at least their new teachers, retorted that they
had not abandoned *the* gospel, only Paul's version of it. Paul

was not swayed. Arrogant as it might sound, Paul insisted that in abandoning his gospel, the Galatians had abandoned *the* gospel, since Paul received his message directly from Jesus. This is the point of Paul's extended discussion of his relations with the Jerusalem church in chapters 1–2: He was emphasizing that his gospel was not from men, just as his apostleship is "not from men, nor through the agency of men, but through Jesus Christ" (1:1, 11–12).

Specifically, the Galatians had abandoned the gospel by seeking to "judaize," that is, to live like Jews. "Troublers" had infiltrated the Galatian church and distorted the gospel (1:7), and 5:1–12 shows that these unknown "troublers" had been preaching that circumcision was necessary for membership in the new covenant. This, Paul says, was simply a denial of the gospel.

Judaizers had even gotten to Peter, though in a somewhat different way. When Peter first arrived to visit the predominately Gentile church in Antioch, he freely shared meals with Gentiles without any care about observing Jewish restrictions on unclean fish or birds, and he ignored all other obstacles to table fellowship. Soon, however, a delegation from the church in Jerusalem arrived, and though they probably did not insist on circumcision and observance of the food laws themselves, they put pressure on Peter to accommodate the Judaizers. Peter buckled and withdrew from table fellowship with Gentiles. This table fellowship might have been a matter of sharing daily meals, but it could also refer to the Lord's Supper. Whichever was the case, when Paul visited Antioch, he confronted Peter sharply in public, accusing him of hypocrisy and insisting that Peter's action was a denial of the gospel, specifically of justification by faith (2:11–21).

Especially for Protestants, Paul's introduction of the

issue of justification in Galatians 2:16 seems irrelevant to the issues under discussion. For us, the doctrine of justification by faith answers the question, "How can a sinner find peace with a holy God?" That was Luther's question, and Luther's answer was the right one: We find peace with God through Jesus, by trusting in Him and not by any moral goodness that we can achieve. But Paul was asking different questions and addressing different issues. His question was, "How are Jewish and Gentile believers related in the church?" And Paul claimed that the doctrine of justification by faith was the answer.

How? Table fellowship has to do with making a covenant, with forming bonds of friendship and communion. Eating with someone shows that we are in a relationship of friendship and peace or that we are forging such a relationship by means of the meal. Because of this, a common meal was often part of covenant-making procedures in biblical times. When Jacob and Laban concluded their "peace treaty," they shared a meal to symbolize their newfound alliance (Genesis 31:54). So also in the Lord's Supper, God invites us to share His table as a sign that we are His friends, that we have peace with Him through Jesus. If sitting down to eat with someone is a sign of covenant relation, then refusing to share a table with someone says, "He is not a friend; he is not at peace with me; I am in no covenant bond with him." When he withdrew from table fellowship with Gentiles, Peter was treating sinners as "sinners," that is, as covenant-breakers.

"Justification," too, is intimately connected with the covenant. In Greek, the word "justify" is related to the word normally translated into English as "righteous," and throughout Scripture, "righteousness" and related words refer to correct behavior within some kind of covenant relationship. Righteousness is conformity to the demands of a covenant. A "righteous" husband is one who meets the obligations of the marriage relationship; a righteous father is one who is faithful to meet the demands of fatherhood; and a righteous civil ruler is one who acts according to the demands of the "social contract." The gospel of Christ is a revelation of God's righteousness because, in Christ, God has fulfilled all the promises made and sworn to Abraham, and thereby has shown that He does what He is obligated to do by His covenant with Israel. In this context, to "justify" someone is to count him as righteous, that is, as a covenant-keeper.

Putting these two things together, we get to the heart of Paul's charge against Peter: Peter was treating the Gentiles as covenant-breakers, as if they were not "righteous," not "justified." Though he might never have consciously decided that the Gentiles were "sinners," Peter's actions spoke clearly enough. Paul caught the drift and charged that Peter had denied justification by faith. Here were Gentiles who believed in Jesus. By Paul's gospel, they were part of God's covenant people, since all who have faith in Jesus are justified and should be treated as covenant-keepers and table fellows. For Paul, what marked the boundaries of table fellowship was the same thing that marked out the justified, and that was and could only be, faith in Jesus. For Peter and the troublers of Galatia, however, faith in Jesus was simply not enough. To the question, "Who is a covenant-keeper?" they answered, "Anyone who believes in Jesus *and also* keeps Jewish food laws, observes Jewish cleanliness regulations, and has been circumcised."

Behind Paul's rebuke is the insight that the doctrine of justification has not only to do with one's individual relationship to God but is an ecclesiological doctrine, having to do with the constitution and shape of the church. Paul insisted that everyone God treats as His friend should be treated as a friend; everyone whom God reckons a covenant-keeper should be welcomed as a covenant-keeper; everyone whom God invites to His table should have a place at the table of the church.

It may seem that we are dealing with historical matters that have little to do with the contemporary Western church but nothing could be further from the truth. The question, "Whom do we treat as God's friends?" is still a central issue, and we have muddled the answer in a way that would have baffled even the Judaizers. We are not tempted to make circumcision or food laws a mark of the covenant, but we have set up other boundaries to fellowship, often subtle and unrecognized but no less wicked for that. In the United States, most churches are racially homogenous (some deliberately so), divided by economic and social status (again, in some cases, deliberately), and separated by political ideology. Instead of being an alternative society, a social space where black and white, employer and employee, Republican and Democrat may fellowship at the one table of the one God, the church mirrors all the divisions of the world.

As if that were not appalling enough, the church adds her own badges of membership to those she borrows from the world. Doctrinal boundaries around the Lord's Supper are necessary, for we are not permitted to welcome Buddhists or Mormons to the Lord's table. But we have established arbitrary doctrinal boundaries. Some Lutheran groups will not allow anyone but Lutherans to share the Lord's table, and these are often synods that consider themselves staunch defenders of the pure gospel of justification by faith. Reformed churches require that a visitor be a member of an "evangelical church" in order to share in the Lord's

Supper: Is there no faith in Christ outside evangelicalism? Other churches permit no one to share the Supper unless he has had a dramatic conversion experience.

Paul would not be impressed.

Access to the Lord's table is not an obscure question of church order, nor am I falling prey to a liberal social gospel when I decry the racial and economic and denominational fragmentation of the church. Paul taught that Peter's practice of denying table fellowship to Gentiles cut to the heart of the gospel because it set up a test of membership other than faith in Jesus and was a fool's bargain in which the gospel was exchanged for something that was no gospel. We must ask ourselves, without evasion or excuse, Have we too been "carried away by hypocrisy" so that we are not "straightforward about the truth of the gospel" (Galatians 2:12–13)?

27

Communion in Christ

Is not the cup of blessing which we bless a sharing in the blood of Christ? Is not the loaf which we break a sharing in the body of Christ? (1 Corinthians 10:16).

The Supper, Martin Luther once wrote, is nothing less than the gospel. Luther meant, primarily, that the Supper is not a human act that makes us acceptable to God, as he believed Zwingli taught, but rather a gift of God. In addition, Luther's insight is based on the more general proposition that the theology of the Supper is the same as the structure of the gospel. To answer the question, What does the Supper mean? we have to answer the prior question, What is the gospel?

Throughout the New Testament, the gospel is an announcement of what God has *done* in Jesus (e.g., Acts 2:14–36). It is not a guide on "how to get saved" but a history lesson, telling the story of Jesus' life, death, resurrection, and ascension. According to the New Testament, through these actions, Jesus inaugurated a new epoch of history, a new order of things. This new age is not just one additional stage in God's dealings with His people but the final and climactic epoch of history, an age that Paul referred to

as the "ends of the ages" (I Corinthians 10:11). The writer
to the Hebrews said that the Lord had revealed Himself
definitively through His Son in "these last days" (Hebrews
1:1–2). When Jesus appeared, an old age waned to be re-
placed by a new.

What especially marks this age from previous ages is
the fact that, through and in Jesus Christ, a new creation
has already begun. The future has become present. Everything that Israel expected to happen at the end of things
has already happened in the middle of things. With Jesus as
the firstfruits, the resurrection of the dead has begun and
Jesus has become the first Man to enter into the new creation (I Corinthians 15:20, 35–49). All those who trust
Him also participate in this new age: "Whoever is in Christ,
there is a new creation" (2 Corinthians 5:17). Though we
have not yet received spiritual bodies, we already share in
the power of Christ's resurrection (Ephesians 1:18–20)
and taste the powers of the age to come. All this is unique
to the Christian age. Prior to the resurrection of Christ,
the new creation was but a distant promise. Now it is a
present reality—a reality only partially manifested but a
present and growing reality nonetheless.

Spartacus was crucified, but his death did not usher in
a new age of history. Lazarus rose from the dead before
Jesus did; why was he not the firstfruits of the resurrection? What makes Christ's death and resurrection unique
is the fact that He was a unique person. He inaugurated
this final, definitive epoch because he was the Last Adam.
Paul expressed this clearly in Romans 5:12–21, where he
described a transition from one "reign" to another: from
the reign of death resulting from sin to the reign of those
who receive the grace of God and the gift of righteousness. It is clear that each reign was established by the

actions of a single man. Through the first Adam came sin, which fulfills itself in death, but through another came the reign of life. Jesus is the Other Man whose actions overturn everything that Adam's actions did. Through His obedience to death, Jesus has brought an end to the old regime and inaugurated a new.

Other contrasts in Paul's writings are best understood as various perspectives on this basic one. To be "fleshly" is to live according to the principles of the Adamic order of sin and death; to be "spiritual" is to be united to the Last Adam who, by His ascension above the firmament, has become, and who gives, the life-giving Spirit (1 Corinthians 15:45). Adam and those who are in him are "of the earth, earthy"; but those who are in Christ live heavenly lives (1 Corinthians 15:47–49; Ephesians 2:6; Colossians 3:1–11). Adamic man exists in a state of living death, while Christian man shares in the life and power of the coming kingdom (Ephesians 2:1–7). Even Paul's contrast between the Old Covenant as a ministry of death and condemnation and the New Covenant as a ministry of life and glory reflects the contrast of Adam and Christ (2 Corinthians 3:1–11).

All this is the New Testament gospel. But how does it affect individual human beings? To be saved means to be delivered from the present evil, Adamic age and transferred into a new age of life, righteousness, and joy. The New Testament describes redemption in many ways: justification, adoption, sanctification, new life, but underlying each of these blessings is the more fundamental reality of union with the exalted Christ. If we are justified, it is because we are joined to the One who was vindicated in His resurrection (Romans 4:25). If we are sons and daughters of God, it is because we are joined to the One who is Eternally the

Son. If we are sanctified, it is because by God's working we are in Christ, and he has become sanctification (1 Corinthians 1:30). If we have new life, it is because we are joined to the One who has been given to have life in Himself (John 5:26). Applied to individual sinners, the gospel is the good news that God has acted to establish a new world and that the blessings and privileges of that world are available to all who will repent and believe.

Against this background, Luther's insight into the nature of the Supper comes clear. Through the bread we break and the cup we bless, we participate in the body and blood of Christ (1 Corinthians 10:16). Because the Supper is a participation in Christ, it is also a participation in all that He, as the Last Adam, has acquired for His people. This is why the New Testament's witness about the Supper is so complex and varied; its benefits are as manifold as the benefits of union to Christ.

The Supper, indeed, is nothing less than the gospel.

28
For You Shall Be Filled

Let us rejoice and be glad and give glory to Him, for the marriage of the Lamb has come and His bride has made herself ready (Revelation 19:7).

Human history begins in hunger, and hunger—whether for bread or for land or for glory or for God—motivates much of that history. Hunger is a sign of our radical dependence, a reminder that we are not autonomous, that we do not share the divine attribute of aseity. Every time the borborygmi thunders in the belly, we are reminded that we need the world if our life is going to continue, and that ultimately we need Life if our life is going to be sustained. Hunger is a constant restlessness. But the Bible does not leave us hungry. It promises filling: "Blessed are you who hunger now, for you shall be satisfied" (Luke 6:21). The Bible does not leave us restless, for there remains a Sabbath rest for the people of God.

Near the close of the Bible is a vision of this rest, this satisfaction, represented, as we have perhaps come to expect, as a feast, in this case a wedding feast. It is a boisterous affair: Revelation 19 begins with a burst of praise, as the multitude in heaven shouts in a loud voice, "Hallelujah! Salvation and glory and power belong to our God."

The saints are celebrating the beginning of the wedding feast, but before that begins, they praise God because He has proven Himself faithful by taking vengeance against the "great harlot who was corrupting the earth with her immorality," whose "smoke rises up forever and ever" (19:2, 4). Everyone in heaven is celebrating the harlot's demise.

And no wonder. This is the harlot who has become drunk on the blood of the saints, the great city that has been filled with the corpses of martyrs. Two millennia into the Christian era, we immediately think that the "great city" is Rome, but in the New Testament, the Jews of Jerusalem were by far the more severe persecutors of the church. According to Jesus' own testimony, not Rome but Jerusalem shed the blood of the prophets and righteous men, and He did not expect her to break this habit when he sent His own prophets and apostles to preach to her (Matthew 23:34–37). Jesus was right. In Acts, a great persecution erupted after the martyrdom of Stephen, and many believers were forced to flee Jerusalem (Acts 7). Shortly after, Saul began ravaging the church under orders from the High Priest, until his dramatic encounter with Jesus on the road to Damascus changed the course of his life and the course of history (Acts 8–9). The rest of the New Testament, then, would lead us to suspect that the city drunk with the blood of the martyrs is Jerusalem.

This suspicion is confirmed by the book of Revelation itself. The harlot is described as the "great city which reigns over the kings of the earth" (17:18), and in 16:19, this same "great city" is called "Babylon the great." Though this too might seem a reference to Rome, Revelation 11:8 puts the matter beyond dispute, since it identifies the city as the one where Jesus was crucified. Revelation is full of sometimes baffling symbolism but it is intended to enlighten, not confuse. If the book defines the "great city" as Jerusalem in chapter eleven, it must be the same city in chapters 17–18. True, the city is called Babylon, Sodom, and Egypt, but those titles tell us something about the spiritual conditions in Jerusalem at the time. If Jerusalem has become a bloodthirsty harlot, the true Israel must flee, following Lot, Moses, Ezra and Nehemiah in an exodus from a doomed city.

In part, too, the saints are celebrating the triumphs of the Man who rides a white horse, who makes war against the kings of the earth (19:11–18). First announced with the outpouring of the sixth bowl (16:12ff), this battle pits the kings who have come west from the Euphrates against the frog-demons. Whether this is a symbolic description of a specific battle, or a general vision of the triumphant church of the New Covenant, it is clear that the one on the white horse is Jesus. His eyes are a flame of fire, as they were in Revelation 1. He is called the "Word of God" (v. 13), a title given to the Son in the first chapter of John's gospel. A sword comes from His mouth, again recalling the description in Revelation 1, and with it He smites the nations and rules them with a rod of iron (see Psalm 2). He is called the King of kings and Lord of lords (v. 16). Jesus is the Head of this army, as He is the Husband of the bride.

As He goes out conquering and to conquer, the corpses of His enemies begin to fill the landscape, and an angel standing in the sun shouts out an invitation to the birds: "Come, assemble for the great supper of God; in order that you may eat the flesh of kings and the flesh of commanders and the flesh of mighty men and the flesh of horses and of those who sit on them and the flesh of all men, both free men and slaves, and small and great" (Revelation 19:17–

18). While the bride feasts with her Husband at her wedding, the birds enjoy a macabre feast on the bodies of those who have been slain by the sword that comes from Christ's mouth.

Jerusalem the harlot first appears riding on the back of the beast, which represents Rome. Jerusalem depends on Rome, but shortly, John predicts, Rome will begin to "hate the harlot and will make her desolate and naked, and will eat her flesh and will burn her up with fire" (17:16). The historical fulfillment of this was the fall of Jerusalem to Roman armies in A.D. 70, and the celebration that takes place in chapter nineteen does not occur at the end of the universe but marks the end of oppressive Jerusalem.

The wedding feast that begins in 19:7 is thus not an eternal feast but begins when the harlot Jerusalem is disposed of. For nineteen hundred years, the church has been celebrating the wedding feast of the Lamb: the harlot is dead; long live the bride. Putting the marriage feast of the Lamb into its biblical context delivers us from any sentimentality with regard to our feast. We get sappy at weddings, but dancing on the grave of a burned harlot is a more solemn affair. Even this is ultimately joyous, and indeed, part of the satisfaction of a wedding feast comes from knowing that God has dealt justly and definitively with His enemies. As in the days of Solomon, our wedding feast is a sign and confession that enemies have been or will be placed beneath His feet. Sobering it may be, but recalling this history is part of the proper celebration of the wedding feast. We are not properly celebrating the feast of the bride unless we are simultaneously celebrating the wake of the harlot.

Though the wedding feast in Revelation 19 does not directly refer to an eternal feast, in the wider biblical context, it is clear that the wedding feast of the Lamb does point ahead to a feast at the end of time. Jesus consistently spoke of the kingdom as a feast, and that is a true description whether we think of the present reality of the kingdom or its future completion. Further, the end of the Old Covenant is a type of the end of all things; just as the old world ended with this double feast, so this whole present world will end in the same manner. Creation week, as Augustine recognized, was a model for this history of man, and both end in Sabbath, in rest and rejoicing.

Man began, each man begins, in hunger, but hunger is not only a sign of dependence. "If there is a natural body, there is also a spiritual body," Paul wrote (1 Corinthians 15:44). And in writing this, he implied that the promise of a spiritual body, a body of the resurrection, was implicit already in the creation of Adam's natural body. Creation implies the completion of creation; protology implies a fulfilled eschatology. Would such a God as this begin a good work without intending to finish it? We may thus infer from Paul that the hunger of Adam is an implicit promise of satisfaction: "If there is hunger, there is filling."

And so it is fitting that the Bible ends where it began, with an invitation to a feast, with the promise of food so satisfying that those who eat and drink shall never hunger nor thirst again.

The Way Things Really Ought To Be: Eucharist, Eschatology, and Culture

For more than half a millennium eucharistic theology con-
ducted its investigations through a zoom lens. The zoom
lens rose to dominance during medieval disputes about the
real presence of Christ's body and blood, and it was further entrenched during Protestant-Catholic disputes on
transubstantiation and intramural Protestant conflicts.[1]
The "zoom lens" metaphor is doubly significant. First, and
here the emphasis is on the "zoom" side of things, for centuries eucharistic theology limited its inquiries to only a
fraction of what takes place in the sacrament. Specifically,

---

[1] On the history of eucharistic theology generally, see Paul H. Jones,
Christ's Eucharistic Presence: A History of the Doctrine (New York: Peter Lang, 1994);
Gary Macy, *The Banquet's Wisdom: A Short History of the Theologies of the Lord's Supper* (New York: Paulist, 1992). On the medieval period, see Henri de Lubac,
Corpus Mysticum: L'eucharistie et l'eglise au moyen age (2d ed.; Paris: Aubier, 1949).
Among many other things, de Lubac traces the gradual transition from understanding the bread as a *sacramentum* of the *corpus ecclesiae* to an understanding in which the bread was identified with the *proprium corpus*, the body born
of the virgin, and a detachment of this hybrid from the ecclesial body. This
led to a shift in attention from the mutually formative relation of church and
Eucharist to questions of the relationship between the *proprium* or *verum corpus* and the *corpus sacramentum*, that is, to questions of substance (e.g., 239).
Recently, some Roman Catholics have expressed doubts about traditional
formulations of transubstantiation. P. J. FitzPatrick (*In Breaking of Bread: The
Eucharist and Ritual* [Cambridge: Cambridge University Press, 1993]), a Roman Catholic priest and professor of philosophy, a self-described "Greek at
the feast," has attacked transubstantiation, as well as such alternatives as
transignification, in language as harsh as any Reformer used. E. Schillebeeckx
and P. Schoonenberg are not dismissive of the traditional teaching but their
efforts at revision show their discomfort with transubstantiation (cf. Jones,
Christ's Eucharistic Presence, 214–231).

debate focused on two issues: what does or does not happen to the bread and wine? And, what benefit does participation in the Eucharist bring to the individual participant? Second, shifting to the "lens" side of things, eucharistic theology was guided by a metaphorical equation of "seeing" and "knowing," a pervasive metaphor in Western philosophy at least since Descartes but one that shaped sacramental theology nearly from the beginning—"visible" words and all that. On this assumption, if the Eucharist does us any good, it is because it "teaches" us something, and if it teaches us something, it is because it "shows" us something.[2]

Liturgical renewal has challenged the zoom focus of the lens in many churches and considerably widened the scope of eucharistic discussion, but within American evangelicalism, the zoom lens continues decisively to shape sacramental theology. For this assertion, I offer two bits of evidence, one textual, the other anecdotal. The textual evidence comes from a systematic theology written by the late Dr. James Montgomery Boice of Tenth Presbyterian Church, Philadelphia. Four elements constitute a sacrament, Boice asserts: it is instituted and commanded by Christ, involves the use of material signs, is a means of grace, and seals and confirms the grace signified. Boice explains the Eucharist in three temporal dimensions: it points to the past atoning death of Jesus, a present personal relationship with Christ, and the future coming of Christ. In explaining the past dimension of the Supper, Boice digresses to reiterate the doctrine of substitutionary atonement; his discussion of the present dimension consists mainly of a

---

[2] For a critique of the risks of the "sight" metaphor for knowledge, see Nicholas Lash, *Easter in Ordinary: Reflections upon Human Experience and the Knowledge of God* (London: SCM Press, 1988) 93–96.

summary of historical debates concerning the real presence; and the hope of Christ's future coming is a comfort for the weary Christian and an encouragement to holiness.[3] Boice's account treats the Supper primarily as an aid to individual spirituality, without a hint of the communal dimensions of the sacrament, and one could read much of Boice's treatment without realizing that the sacrament under discussion is a *meal*. When Boice is not discussing the benefits of the Supper for the individual believer, he is rehashing Reformation debates about the metaphysics of the bread and wine.

My anecdotal evidence comes from my experience in the Presbyterian Church in America (PCA), in which I hold my ordination. A typical PCA ordination exam includes only one question on the Lord's Supper: "Name and define the four views of the Lord's Supper," the "four views" being transubstantiation, consubstantiation, memorialist, and Calvinist. In my admittedly limited experience, there is no recognition that these four theories were formulated in response to a small set of questions nor that these four views do not exhaust the possible answers even to the question of substance.

Though these bits of evidence are hardly a demonstration, they, together with an array of impressions, experiences, anecdotes, and texts, lead me to this conclusion: defining the substance of the elements and their relation to the natural body of Christ—especially, defining that relation, according to a kind of *via negativa*, over against the

[3] James Montgomery Boice, *Foundations of Christian Faith: A Comprehensive and Readable Theology* (Downers Grove: InterVarsity, 1986) 595–605. The popular character of this text makes it particularly useful for my purposes, since what Boice explains here is presumably what he would want the "man in the pew" to know of sacramental theology.

Roman Catholic doctrine—is the alpha and omega of evangelical eucharistic theology. This is eucharistic theology with a zoom lens as narrowly focused as anything in medieval theology, perpetuated in a sector of American Christianity that (often ignorantly) holds the medieval church in contempt.

A completely different picture emerges when the camera is drawn back and we examine the Eucharist through a wide-angle lens. Instead of attending only to bread and wine on a table, we see people and they are doing things. They are not simply observing the elements but passing them from hand to hand, sharing them, eating and drinking them. Words are being spoken. In most churches, one or a few members of the congregation stand nearer the "elements," while the rest sit, stand, or kneel at a greater distance, revealing a hierarchy of some kind. Through the zoom lens, the Eucharist is presented as a miraculous puzzle of physics or metaphysics; through a wide-angle lens, the Eucharist becomes a focal point for more theologically central issues: the relationships of the church's members to one another, creation, and God. It will be noted here that I have simply changed lenses, rather than providing a wholly different technology; most of this paper attacks the "zoom" rather than the "lens" of eucharistic reflection. That is a first step, and, I think, an important one, but I will return at the end of this article to the "problem of the lens," for it seems to me the only way to formulate a satisfying sacramental theology and practice is a thoroughgoing demolition of all lenses and the discovery of a sounder metaphorical apparatus.

Before filling in this sketch of a wide-angle view of the Eucharist, I will set my concerns in a larger context. First, the anthropological subdiscipline of ritual theory has

explored how rituals express, reinforce, and even constitute the values and structures of a community,[4] and several recent studies bring these anthropological insights to
bear on sacramental theology.[5] Several scholars have ob-
jected to current formulations of ritual theory, and there
are also theological problems.[6] Anthropologists, for example, deliberately use "ritual" to blur distinctions between
worship and idolatry or between prayer and magic, distinctions that are fundamental to Christian theology.[7] To be
sure, similarities exist between the table of the Lord and
the table of demons, since both are food rites, but a radical
antithesis overshadows them.

Despite well-founded objections, ritual theory can serve
as a useful corrective to the myopia of some sacramental
theology. Evangelical Protestants frequently treat sacraments, despite their location in the textbooks, exclusively
in the context of individual soteriology. The central

[4] See, for example, Mary Douglas, *Natural Symbols: Explorations in Cosmol-
ogy* (2d ed.; London: Barries and Jenkins, 1973); Victor Turner, *The Ritual Process:
Structure and Anti-Structure* (Chicago: Aldine, 1966); E. Leach, *Culture and Communication* (Cambridge: Cambridge University Press, 1976).

[5] Bernard Cooke, *The Distancing of God: The Ambiguity of Symbol in History and
Theology* (Minneapolis: Fortress, 1990); Michael G. Lawler, *Symbol and Sacra-
ment: A Contemporary Sacramental Theology* (New York: Paulist, 1987); Joseph J.
Schaller, "Performative Language Theory: An Exercise in the Analysis of Ritual,"
Worship 62:5 (September 1988) 415–432; E. Byron Anderson, "Performance,
Practice and Meaning in Christian Baptism," *Worship* 69:6 (November 1995)
482–504.

[6] Douglas, for example, presumes a Durkheimian framework in her efforts to trace, in a rather direct fashion, the lines connecting social structure
and ritual. For a critique of Durkheim from a theological angle, see John
Milbank, *Theology and Social Theory: Beyond Secular Reason* (Oxford: Blackwell, 1990),
61–71.

[7] According to Jack Goody, A. R. Radcliffe Brown used "ritual" in a way
that embraced both religion and magic so as to avoid the classic anthropological problem of defining the boundaries between the two ("Religion and
Ritual: The Definitional Problem," *British Journal of Sociology* 12 [1961] 147).

question has been, How is grace conveyed through my participation in the elements of the sacrament? What can the sacraments do *for me*? Ritual theory, by contrast, explores rites in relation to the faith and practices of the communities that celebrate and enact them; in theological terms, ritual theory situates sacramental and liturgical theology firmly within ecclesiology and thus forces upon us such questions as, What do the rites of the church express about the church's understanding of herself, her place in the world, and of the human vocation? How are her rites not only means of grace to the individual participant but also formative of the church's communal ethos and interpersonal relations? Ritual theory thus helps sacramental theology break the frame of the zoom lens.

Second, ritual theory gives prominence to the significance of ritual action and thus challenges some common definitions of sacrament. Sacraments, according to a venerable formulation that goes back to Augustine, emerge at the intersection of the Word and the physical elements of bread, wine, or water.[8] Even if we (rightly) insist that the

---

[8] Nicholas Lash states that in traditional Roman Catholic sacramental theology, the *materia* is an action and never simply a thing (*His Presence in the World: A Study of Eucharistic Worship and Theology* [London: Sheed & Ward, 1968] 46). If true, this would exempt Catholic theology of the criticisms brought forward in this paragraph. De Lubac offers evidence that this was indeed the case among many medieval theologians, but it does not seem to have been universal. For Peter the Lombard (*Sentences* 4.3.1.2; PL 192, 843), baptism is an *intinctio, id est ablutio corporis exterior, facta sub forma verborum praescripta. Si enim fiat ablutio sine verbo, non est ibi sacramentum; sed accedente verbo ad elementum, fit sacramentum, non utique ipsum elementum fit sacramentum, sed ablutio facta in elemento*, a formulation that explicitly states that the *elementum* to which the word is added is the *ablutio* and not water *simpliciter*. The situation, however, is less clear for Thomas Aquinas. In explaining why words are added to the elements of the sacraments, he states that the material (*res*) of the sacraments includes *actus sensibiles* such as washing and anointing (*Summa Theologiae* 3a.60.6) but, on the other hand, in discussing the Eucharist, he asks whether bread and wine are properly the *materia* of the Eucharist (3a.74.1) and reserves discussion of the

word is not a magic incantation but the word preached and believed, this definition is still terribly inadequate. Water in the presence of the word preached does not make baptism; bread and wine over which the words of institution are spoken do not make the Eucharist. A definition of the Eucharist limited to the two factors of element (or object) and word presses toward something like an iconic view of the sacramental elements, in which the elements, apart from their use as food, are understood as communicators of grace. Images such as "mirrors" and "pictures" suffer the same flaws and produce a sacramental theology heavy on the lens.[9] Even Augustine's apparently innocuous and oft-repeated claim that sacraments are *sacra signa* or "symbols" can imply that they exist to be *viewed* and thus can tilt sacramental theology toward the worst abuses of medieval theory and practice. At the least, defining sacraments as "signs" often carries intellectualist freight, so that the sacraments come to be understood as material for contemplation or visual aids to teaching—"God's flannel graph," as Richard B. Gaffin put it in a conversation. Combined with a focus on the question of what happens to the eucharistic elements, such definitions and metaphors institutionalize the zoom lens.

---

ritus of the Eucharist to a later section (3a.83). In 74.6, he explicitly states that *aqua est materia baptismi* and *panis et vinum sunt materia hujus sacramenti*. Among evangelical writers, Boice identifies water, bread, and wine as the material elements of the sacraments (*Foundations of the Christian Faith*, 595), while Berkhof more helpfully includes the "sacred rite" with the physical objects as part of the *materia externa* of the sacraments (*Systematic Theology* [Grand Rapids: Eerdmans, 1953] 617).

[9] Visual images are abundant in Calvin's discussion of "sacraments in general." Cf. *Institutes of the Christian Religion* (Library of Christian Classics, #21; 2 vols.; ed. John T. McNeill; trans. Ford Lewis Battles; Philadelphia: Westminster, 1960) 4.14.5–6.

Lacking in these definitions and metaphors is a clear indication that a sacrament requires actions and people, as well as words and material objects. Baptism is not water plus preaching, but water that an officiant applies to a subject in the Name of the Trinity; the Eucharist is not the word plus bread and wine, but the word plus the bread and wine eaten and drunk by the gathered people of God. Action and congregation are constituent factors of the sacraments and must be included in any adequate definition or theological reflection. Once the necessity of communal action is accepted, it is apparent that the terms "rite" and "ritual" are more adequate one-word descriptions of sacraments than "symbols" or "signs," and this in turn suggests further possibilities for interaction between sacramental theology and ritual theory.

A final preliminary point: once sacramental theology has been genuinely situated in ecclesiology, it becomes apparent that the sacraments are inseparable from the mission of the church and the church's relationship to the world in such a way that we can consider sacramental theology as an aspect and a way of examining the church's relationship to culture. One may fruitfully examine this relationship from the perspective that the church is a distinct culture, "culture" here being defined in the expansive anthropological sense as the beliefs, values, practices—the whole way of life—of an organized group.[10] As a distinct culture, the church has a twofold mission: to maintain the symbolic boundaries that separate her from worldly culture and to seek to form the surrounding culture into something like the culture that exists within the church.

[10] I have found George Lindbeck's use of a "cultural-linguistic" framework for comparative religions useful. See *The Nature of Doctrine: Religion and Theology in a Postliberal Age* (London: SPCK, 1984) 32–42.

The ways in which the church is a distinct culture may be specified by reference to the Protestant doctrine of the marks or notes of the church: word, sacrament, and discipline.[11] Protestant theologians have used these notes to distinguish true from false churches but I am using them to identify how the church is distinguished from the world and to explain the specific ways in which the church seeks to remake the world. To say that the church is a culture in respect of the "word" is to say that the members of the church find their individual and communal identity by reference to the narrative summarized in the creeds, that they speak a language distinct from that of the world, one rooted in and shaped by the revelation given in the Bible, and therefore that they conceptualize and order reality in conformity with the biblical pattern of language. The church's mission in respect to the word is to proclaim the story of sin and redemption, to seek to make the Christian language the dominant language of culture, and to persuade individuals and nations to find their purpose within the history of the Christian gospel. To say that the church is a culture in respect of "discipline" means that the church defines and maintains Christian moral boundaries,[12] and her mission

[11] These three marks are not sharply distinct, and each can be understood to imply the others. A church marked by the word will celebrate the rites of the church and exercise the ministry of the keys; a church that faithfully celebrates Christ's sacraments will do so in obedience to the Word and will guard the sacraments from profanation by flagrant sinners; a church that exercises discipline does so according to the law of Christ, and this discipline has its focus in access to the Eucharist. The three marks are "perspectivally related" in the sense used by John Frame, *Doctrine of the Knowledge of God* (Phillipsburg: Presbyterian & Reformed, 1987).

[12] See Philip Rieff, *The Feeling Intellect: Selected Writings* (Chicago: University of Chicago Press, 1990) 273–90. Rieff argues that culture is founded on the "primacy of interdiction," on the "thou shalt nots," which are enforced and passed on to the next generation by a "priesthood."

in respect of discipline is to see her moral boundaries honored in the wider culture so that Christian norms become the foundation of social custom and even law. To say that the church is a culture in respect to "sacraments" suggests that the church's rites express her understanding of reality and her place in it and challenge the world's conceptions of her and of itself. How this is the case is the subject of the next two sections.

I. Eucharist and Eschatology[13]

According to the Bible, the kingdom of God is the creation renewed and brought to its intended end. Through His redemptive work in Christ, God will bring the world to a condition of cosmic peace, of *shalom*, of harmony among God, man, and the creation. Adam's sin spoiled the harmonious goodness of the original creation, but, through Jesus, the Last Adam and Prince of Peace, God intends to put things in their proper place. The renewal of the creation is to be understood in the eschatological "already-not yet" framework that shapes New Testament theology as a whole. The gospel of the resurrection means not only that dead Jesus came back to life (though it means that) but also that Jesus has entered the realm of life, of the new creation and of the Spirit. In him, the new creation has already begun and the kingdom has been established, though the creation is not yet fully renewed, restored, or transfigured into a new heavens and a new earth. Only by faith does the believer know that, through his death and resurrection, Jesus

[13] See Geoffrey Wainwright, *Eucharist and Eschatology* (New York: Oxford University Press, 1981). I have explored these themes at greater length in *The Kingdom and the Power: Rediscovering the Centrality of the Church* (Phillipsburg: P&R, 1993) 107–126.

fundamentally renovated the world but his resurrection and ascension guarantee that he will in the end bring the world to its destined fulfillment.

Especially in Jesus' teaching, the renewed and fulfilled creation that is the kingdom of God takes the specific form of a feast. Jesus used the image of the feast more than any other to describe the reality of his kingdom. He promised the disciples they would sit on thrones and have table fellowship in the kingdom (Luke 22:28–30), told the believing centurion that many would come from the east and west to recline at the table with Abraham, Isaac, and Jacob in the kingdom (Matthew 8:5–13), and told the parable of a king inviting reluctant guests to a banquet (Matthew 22:1–14). When John the Baptist wanted to distinguish his ministry from that of Jesus, he called Jesus the Bridegroom whose coming marked the beginning of the joyful wedding celebration (John 3:29; cf. 2:1–11). The omega point toward which history is moving is the wedding feast of the Lamb, the concrete embodiment of eschatological *shalom*. In short, this is the way the world ends: with neither bang nor whimper but with the laughter of a wedding feast.

On the night in which He instituted His Supper, Jesus spoke of the Eucharist directly in relation to the future feast of the kingdom: "I will not drink of this fruit of the vine from now on until that day when I drink it new with you in My Father's kingdom" (Matthew 26:29). As Paul said, in the Supper the church "proclaims Jesus' death until He comes" (1 Corinthians 11:26), thus placing the Supper within an eschatological horizon. The Eucharist is the now of the feast of the end of the age, a "foretaste" of the future celebration. Because the Bridegroom has come, He offers the wedding feast now, and, though the feast the church celebrates is perhaps only a crumb or two from the table, it is a real anticipation of that future feast.

If the kingdom is the creation pacified and transfigured, if the renewed creation takes the form of a banquet, and if the Eucharist is a proleptic celebration of the feast of the kingdom—if all this is true, the Eucharist should be understood as a sign of the renewed creation. The Eucharist is our model of the eschatological order, a microcosm of the way things really ought to be.

II. *The Way Things Really Ought To Be*

In considering how the Eucharist previews the kingdom, the eschatological order of *shalom*, the zoom lens is a distraction, not an aid. The character of the kingdom is revealed not in a substantial transformation of bread and wine, or in the absence of such a transformation, or in a believer's individual communion, but in the whole action of the common meal. The question addressed below is, What vision of human life emerges from a wide-angle consideration of the Eucharist? In the following reflections, I deliberately avoid most of the technical terminology of traditional eucharistic theology. Discourses in a philosophical key are worthwhile but there is also value in playing in a more directly biblical mode. One of the consistent errors of sacramental theology, moreover, has been its confusion, as P. J. FitzPatrick has put it, of signs and disguises,[14] which has led to the assumption that one can unveil the meaning of the Eucharist only by penetrating beneath the surface to a metaphysical reality available only to intellect or faith. Jesus' "This is My Body" indicates that more is going on than any lens can capture, but efforts to penetrate disguises can skim too lightly over the surface and

[14] *In Breaking of Bread*, 133–74.

miss the obvious. To avoid the confusion of signs and disguises, the following reflections linger on what can loosely be called a phenomenological level of analysis. "Deeper" issues will be discussed, but here the first question will be, What vision of human life emerges from reflection on the *surface* of the eucharistic rite?[15]

Obviously, the Eucharist is a meal; at the Lord's table, we *eat*.[16] Eating models the way things really ought to be, the order of the final kingdom of God that is already, though only in part, a reality on earth. How? It is significant that Jesus chose as the sacrament of His kingdom one of the most common of human activities. The Eucharist is different from the common meals of daily life, but it is also continuous with them. This suggests that the kingdom does not involve a cancellation of this-worldly concerns; it is not a another world but rather *this* world transformed and transfigured. As Russian Orthodox liturgist Alexander Schmemann constantly insisted, the Eucharist shows us that the world of eating and drinking—which means, as we will see, the world of work and exchange, of family and friends, of politics and power—is the matter from which God shapes His kingdom.[17]

Eating reveals humanity's place in the cosmos by

[15] This is a reversion to an ancient mode of sacramental theology. The theologically interesting portions of Tertullian's *De baptismo* are meditations on the biblical imagery and natural properties of water, and the *Didache's* (9) interpretation of the eucharistic bread, made of seeds gathered from many fields, as a symbol of the gathered church, was incorporated into the *Glossa Ordinaria* on 1 Cor 10:17 (cited by Thomas, *Summa Theologiae* 3a.74.1, who also cites Augustine, *In Johannem* 6.56). Likewise, Thomas consistently seeks to relate the natural properties of the symbols and actions of the sacraments to their theological significance.

[16] Much of the material below was inspired by Leon R. Kass, Jr., *The Hungry Soul: Eating and the Perfecting of our Nature* (New York: Free Press, 1994).

[17] See especially, Schmemann, *For the Life of the World: Sacraments and Orthodoxy* (Crestwood: St. Vladimir's Seminary Press, 1973).

expressing our creatureliness. Creatures have no life in them-, selves but must take in fuel from outside to live. Man's need for food is a memorial of his dependence upon creation and thus manifests our symbiotic embeddedness in the world.[18] Ultimately, however, creatures do not derive life from the creation. Food is dead, and dead matter cannot give life. Calvin wrote that Jesus' (and before Him, Moses') claim that "man does not live by bread alone" is literally true.[19] We are genuinely dependent upon bread as a secondary cause," but bread can give life only through the power of the Creator, the Spirit who is the Lord and Giver of Life.

Eating also signifies humanity's dominion over the creation. When I eat, I incorporate a part of the world into myself, and therefore to eat a once-living thing is to say that its life is rightly subordinate to my needs, that it exists (at least in part) to serve and sustain me, that I have a right to make it mine in the most literal and intimate sense. Throughout the food chain, to eat something is to claim superiority over it: herbivorous animals eat what is lower on the chain, while more complicated and advanced animals eat lower animals. The exceptions to this rule—man-eating lions, cannibals, Polyphemus—are horrific not only for their goriness but because they disturb our sense of right order. At the top of the food chain is man, anatomically

---

[18] One of the great contributions of Orthodox liturgics is its emphasis on the cosmic and environmental dimensions of the Eucharist. See the discussion of John Zizioulas in Paul McPartland, *The Eucharist Makes the Church: Henri de Lubac and John Zizioulas in Dialogue* (Edinburgh: T&T Clark, 1993); Zizioulas, *Being is Communion: Studies in Personhood and the Church* (London: Darton, Longman and Todd, 1985); Schmemann, *For the Life*.

[19] *Institutes* 1.16.7; 3.20.44. See James B. Jordan, "The Meaning of Eating in the Bible" (Studies in Food and Faith, #7; Niceville: Biblical Horizons, 1990) 1–5.

equipped, as Leon Kass has pointed out, to eat nearly everything. Kass writes that humanity's place in the food chain is a sign both of proper dominion and of the potential for irresponsible domination:

> The expansion and indeterminacy of human appetites—reflected in human omnivorousness—are greatly problematic, as is man himself. . . . Human omnivorousness is the bodily mark of man . . . as deformer and transformer. It is the unpremeditated, strictly natural sign of our dominant and mastering posture in the world, a posture of great danger as well as great promise, not only for the world but also for man himself.[20]

Several passages in the Bible show this connection between eating and authority. In Genesis 2:16–17, the Lord grants Adam the world to eat, while in Genesis 1:26–28, He presents the world to man and woman as the domain they are to fill, subdue, and rule. To be made in God's image means not only to be given every herb for food but also to be given dominion over the earth and other living creatures. After the flood, the Lord's promises to the new Adam, Noah, bring dominion even more directly into connection with diet:

> And God blessed Noah and his sons and said to them, "Be fruitful, multiply, and fill the earth. And the fear of you and the terror of you shall be on every beast of the earth and on every bird of the sky; with everything that creeps on the ground, and all the fish of the sea, into your hand they are given. Every moving thing that is alive shall be food

[20] Kass, *The Hungry Soul*, 92.

for you; I give all to you, as I gave the green plant"
(Genesis 9:1–3).

God promises effective rule over animals at the same time
he gives permission to eat flesh.[21]

As a preview of the *shalom* of the new creation, the Eucharist manifests man's proper place in the creation and
his relation to what we must insist on calling the lower
creation. Much more than Christian theology has recognized that man is part of and inseparable from the created
order, inserted into his environment, shaped by it, dependent upon what it offers, and responsible for its care. God
also created man as the omnivorous ruler of the world, to
whom every tree, as well as every beast and creeping thing,
is edible. Man's position as ruler is part of the creation
order that God pronounced "very good," not a part of the
curse on sin, and the new creation brings fulfillment, not a
cancellation of his position. One could tease out a Christian environmental theology from such reflections on eating, and it would be useful to explore if or how the tension
might be resolved eucharistically.

The Eucharist depicts the world as it really ought to
be: at the Lord's table, we eat *bread*. Debates about the physics
of the bread have so dominated eucharistic theology for
several centuries that the simple fact that Jesus chose bread
has received little attention. Jesus could have instituted a
ritual meal using roasted grain or red meat, which were used

---

[21] By way of contrast, it is significant that the feast of the new creation
involves only vegetable fare. I would not wish to use this to make a case for
vegetarianism, but the food of the Eucharist seems to reflect biblical prophecies
that the new creation will bring not merely peace *from* animals but peace *between* man and the animals. On the place of animals in the covenant, see Robert
Murray, *The Cosmic Covenant: Biblical Themes of Justice, Peace and the Integrity of Creation* (London: Sheed and Ward, 1992), chapters 6–7.

in Old Testament feasts, but he chose to signify the kingdom with a feast of bread. That Jesus took bread—the universal staple of human diet—reinforces the nature of the kingdom as a transformation of this world, as a glorification of the creature, rather than an elevation of man above creatureliness. Renewed humanity does not consume ambrosia; mundane though it may be, the kingdom of heaven is populated by bread-eaters. Beyond that, Jesus chose a food that does not occur naturally.[22] Bread is a uniquely human food; as Samuel Johnson observed, animals think and feel but no beast is a cook. Bread production is thus a further clue to the Christian conception of man's place in the creation. To invent bread, Kass notes, one must apply a complex set of discoveries and operations that transforms wheat from its natural state:

> Human beings must discover that certain harvestable and storable but inedible seeds, if ground, will yield flour, which, if moistened, can be kneaded into dough, which, if baked, becomes an edible, relatively nonspoilable product. . . . Next are the various arts of agriculture, from plowing, fertilizing, and sowing to irrigating, harvesting, and storing— many of which involve other arts, such as metalworking, toolmaking, and animal taming.[23]

When bread is set on the table, an agricultural and culinary science and technology lies in the background. Breadmaking man is thus set over the creation, to borrow the term used by James B. Jordan, as the agent of transforma-

---

[22] None of the various grain or "tribute" offerings (minchah) of Leviticus 2 prescribe raw grains; at the least the grain was roasted; at most it was baked into unleavened cakes.

[23] Kass, *The Hungry Soul*, 121.

tion and transfiguration.[24] Mankind is given the creation
not only to use its products in their natural state but also
to transform them for the enrichment of human life; he is
not only guardian of what is but is creator of what is not
yet; mankind is not only to eat but to bake. The bread-
maker is the creature who builds cities, sends probes to the
edges of the galaxy, transforms sand into silicon chips. Bread-
making humanity is scientific and technological humanity.
We have here not only the beginnings of a eucharistic theology of technology but also the beginnings of a eucharistic aesthetics.

And a eucharistic economics is implicit in the choice
of bread. Kass points out that bread production requires
the presence of certain moral-cultural, social, political, and
economic conditions:

> Men must be willing to settle down and remain at-
> tached to a particular place, and an open and ex-
> posed place at that. Their natural indolence and their
> desire for prompt satisfaction of need must be
> overcome. Men must be able to plan for and an-
> ticipate the future, and be willing to defer gratifi-
> cation, in order to accept as a regular way of life
> laboring today for a goal far in the future. . . . With
> agriculture a new human relationship to nature and
> to fellow man emerges: . . . There is the nascent
> idea of ownership, of property in nature, perhaps
> tied to the admixture of one's own labor, first to
> the agricultural produce and then to the soil; the
> idea of appropriation eventually makes necessary
> rules of justice, governing what is mine and thine,

[24] Jordan, *Through New Eyes: Developing a Biblical View of the World* (Nashville:
Wolgemuth & Hyatt, 1989) 133–141.

and points to new and more complex social arrange-
ments. . . . A transformer of nature, a practitioner
of art, a restrainer of his own appetites, a settled
social creature soon with laws and rules of justice,
poised proudly yet apprehensively between the earth
and the cosmic powers—man becomes human with
the eating of bread.[25]

When Jesus offered bread at his feast, he was taking up
this whole system into the kingdom as well. If Kass is correct that bread production requires these institutional structures, and if Jesus made use of the product of these
structures, then He can hardly have rejected them in principle. The kingdom of heaven is not Rousseau's primeval
state of equality; by making bread, and hence the political
economy of bread production, part of the model of the
way things really ought to be, Jesus endorsed the distinction of *meum* and *tuum* as an aspect of redeemed life.

At the Lord's table, we eat bread and *drink wine*. Kass's
comments about bread apply here as well, for Jesus did not
give His disciples grapes, but the blood of the grape, which
is the creation transformed by human creativity and labor.
Like bread, wine assumes a degree of technological sophis-
tication, as well as a measure of social and political formation. Wine, however, is a drink of celebration and not mere
nutrition. If Jesus had wanted to depict man's relation to
creation and to God in purely utilitarian terms, bread and
water would have sufficed. This Bridegroom, however,
changes water to wine, and in so doing, clarifies man's purpose in the world. In a famous rhetorical flourish, dour old
Calvin claimed that the very structure of creation indicates
it exists to be enjoyed not merely used:

[25] Kass, *The Hungry Soul*, 121–122.

[T]he natural qualities themselves of things demonstrate sufficiently to what end and extent we may
enjoy them. Has the Lord clothed the flowers with
the great beauty that greets our eyes, the sweetness of smell that is wafted upon our nostrils, and
yet will it be unlawful for our eyes to be affected
by that beauty, or our sense of smell by the sweetness of that odor? What? Did he not so distinguish colors as to make some more lovely than
others? What? Did he not endow gold and silver,
ivory and marble, with a loveliness that renders them
more precious than other metals or stones? Did he
not, in short, render many things attractive to us,
apart from their necessary use?[26]

The vision of life implied by the wine of the Eucharist
is what John Schneider has called "godly materialism," a
vision of "productive work, abundance, flourishing and delight" in the creation.[27]

In biblical perspective, the use of wine in the Eucharist
has additional significance. Under Levitical law, drinking
wine in the immediate presence of God was strictly forbidden (Leviticus 10:9). As Jordan has argued, the reason for
this prohibition lies in the sabbatical and eschatological nature
of wine. Wine induces relaxation and so is appropriate as
Sabbath drink, but the priests of Israel, who alone had access to the Holy Place, never did relax while they minis-
tered, as a sign, as the book of Hebrews points out, that
the blood of bulls and goats did not atone for sin (Hebrews 10:11–14). No one enjoyed full Sabbath under the
terms of the old covenant. With the coming of a new and

[26] *Institutes* 3.10.2.

[27] John Schneider, *Godly Materialism* (Downers Grove: InterVarsity).

better covenant in Jesus, however, wine is not only permitted but required in God's presence. Jesus, the high priest of the order of Melchizedek, has completed His work, and therefore He can sabbath before his Father; better blood has been shed, so the Lord invites His people to a feast of wine in His presence. Because wine is sabbatical, it is also eschatological. Wine is offered at the end of the day, when the bread-making work is done, not at its beginning. Making wine, moreover, takes time; wine must age and mature before it can be enjoyed. There is a profound theological truth in the old advertizing slogan, "We will sell no wine before it's time." The eucharistic wine proclaims the New Testament gospel of the kingdom: "The time is fulfilled, the kingdom of heaven is at hand."[28]

At the Lord's table, *we* eat bread and drink wine *together*. And this is the way things ought to be: the ideal world is not a world of atomized individuals but an irreducibly social reality. Biological need can be satisfied in isolation; we can eat in the car, at a desk, in front of a computer screen, but a feast is a social event. Alongside the eucharistic ecology and economics sketched above, we discover a eucharistic sociology, which is to say, an ecclesiology. Because we eat together of one loaf, we are one Body, members not only of Christ but of one another (1 Corinthians 10:17), called to radical Christlike, self-sacrificing love, to use whatever gifts we have for the edification of the Body, to lives of forbearance, forgiveness, and peace. This eucharistic sociology significantly qualifies the eucharistic economics. While the distinction of *meum* and *tuum* is

---

[28] For more extensive reflections on the theology of wine, see Jeffrey J. Meyers, "Concerning Wine and Beer," *Rite Reasons* 48–49 (November 1996/January 1997).

not dissolved, the Eucharist ritually manifests the Christian's calling to use what is his, both wealth and gifts, for the good of the whole Body.

The Body is not without order; again, the kingdom of God is not a Rousseauian paradise. In most churches, only ordained ministers may administer the Supper, and even if this is an unnecessary remnant of clericalism, it is still true that in all properly functioning churches of Christ some-one is designated as guardian of the table. Flagrant and impenitent sinners are to be cut off from the fellowship of the feast. In this way, the Eucharist not only manifests and exercises proper relationships among the members of the Body but also reveals the fundamental contours of the world as a whole. And not only "reveals": Since the exercise of church discipline centers on the table, the feast *establishes* boundaries, creating an in-group and an out-group. Those who participate in the feast are members of the Body, to be treated as brothers and sisters, while those outside may be enemies of the church, apostates cut off from Christ, or the unevangelized. The feast draws the ever-shifting lines between the church and the world.

At the Lord's table, we eat bread and drink wine to-gether, *with thanksgiving*. Redeemed man is called not only to dominion, to kingship, but also to priesthood. Our do-minion is in service to priestly worship, since we engage in the royal labor of baking bread and crushing grapes—that is, we construct culture—in order to celebrate with our labor's produce in worship before the Lord. As Schmemann explains,

> The first, the basic definition of man is that he is
> *the priest*. He stands in the center of the world and
> unifies it in his act of blessing God, of both re-

ceiving the world from God and offering it to God—
and by filling the world with this Eucharist, he transforms his life, the one that he receives from the
world, into life in God, into communion with Him.
The world was created as the "matter," the material of one all-embracing Eucharist, and man was
created as the priest of this cosmic sacrament.[29]

At the Lord's table, we eat bread and drink wine together *to proclaim the Lord's death until He comes.* Here, a wide-
angle exploration of the Eucharist casts fresh light on one
of the traditional, "deeper" questions of eucharistic and
liturgical theology. Paul writes that the Supper proclaims
the death of Jesus until He comes (1 Corinthians 11:26),
but how is this the case? Liturgists have sometimes attempted
to locate some act in the rite of the Supper that corre-
sponds to the death of Jesus: Some suggest the fraction
(breaking of bread) correlates with the breaking of Jesus'
body, while others note the separation of bread and wine as
a sign of sacrificial death, while others refer this to the
repetition of the words of institution. I find these efforts
strained, since it is all but impossible to make a meal look
like a death by crucifixion. Breaking bread and pouring out
wine has, by an act of imaginative faith, been understood
as an enactment of the crucifixion, but more appropriate
media for such a portrayal are conceivable, as Thomas Aquinas
recognized: *Carnes animalium occisorum expresse repraesentent Christi
passionem.*[30] More seriously, these efforts assume, as Paul
H. Jones put it, that the "root metaphor" of the Eucharist
is "tomb" rather than "table,"[31] an assumption that has

---

[29] *For the Life of the World,* 15.

[30] *Summa Theologiae* 3a.74.1.

[31] Jones, *Christ's Eucharistic Presence,* 45.

blossomed in all manner of bizarre eucharistic mischief. The Eucharist is not, in short, a passion play.

And yet the Supper proclaims the Lord's death. Once we have broken free of the limitations of the zoom lens, however, there is no reason to assume that the proclamation takes place by the minister's manipulation of the elements. Since the Supper is the communal meal as a whole, the fact that we eat together and the way we do it, *that* is what "proclaims the Lord's death." There are good exegetical reasons for believing that this is what Paul meant. First, "eating and drinking" is precisely what, according to Paul, proclaims the Lord's death (I Corinthians 11:26): not the fraction, the pouring of wine, or the words of institution but the common meal. We get a further clue from Paul's striking charge in 11:20 that when the Corinthians came together it was *not* to eat the Lord's Supper. It is not going too far to suggest that, for Paul, the Corinthian meals, since they were not the Lord's Supper, did not proclaim the Lord's death. Whatever words were said and whatever actions performed, the Corinthians did not truly show the death of Christ in their gatherings. Why not? The meals the Corinthians held were not celebrations of the Supper because factions divided the church, because members were acting selfishly, and because, by these sinful actions, they had divided the indivisible Christ (1:10–13; 11:17–22). The difference between the Lord's Supper and its perversion does not consist in any difference in the ritual actions, the elements used, or the words spoken but rather lies in the way people behave toward one another. The Lord's death is proclaimed only when the church celebrates rightly, that is, when Christian peace, love, and unity are manifested in the meal, and when their conduct at the meal fits the way the community lives together.

A "wide angle" consideration of the Eucharist as a sacrificial meal supports this conclusion. Any mention of sacrifice in connection with the Supper raises the specter of Roman Catholicism, but I reject the Roman view, not only for the reasons that Protestants have traditionally brought forward but also because the Roman Catholic view, by concentrating on what the priest does at the altar, is the textbook example of the distortions of the "zoom lens." This does not mean, however, that the Supper is in no sense a sacrificial meal. Like the sacrificial meals of the Old Testament, it involves eating the flesh of a substitutionary victim; the bread and wine are called "body and blood," sacrificial terms if ever there were any; the Supper is the Christian Passover (1 Corinthians 5:7), and the Passover was clearly a sacrificial meal. Recognizing a sacrificial dimension in the Supper has reasonable precedent in Reformed theology. Pierre du Moulin, a French Reformed pastor, enumerated in 1635 the "particular reasons for calling the Eucharist a sacrifice":

> I. Because this sacrament was instituted to proclaim the Lord's death until He come. . . . Hence the Eucharist may be called a sacrifice, since it represents the sacrifice of the Lord's death. According to the principle that signs and representations ordinarily take the name of that which they signify. II. It may be said that in the Eucharist we offer Jesus Christ to God, insofar as we ask God to receive on our behalf the sacrifice of His death. III. The Eucharist is a sacrifice of thanksgiving for the divine benefits and especially for the benefit of our redemption through Jesus Christ.

Du Moulin distinguished propitiatory sacrifices from

sacrifices of thanksgiving, and, though he said that in a certain sense the Eucharist is a propitiatory sacrifice (since it commemorates a propitiatory sacrifice), he insisted that, strictly speaking, it is a sacrifice of thanksgiving. "Thus the Eucharist may be a sacrament insofar as by it God gives us and conveys His grace, and a sacrifice insofar as we offer Him our praise and thanksgiving."[32]

In *Civitatis Dei* 10.5, Augustine makes several comments about sacrifice that point to another sense in which the eucharistic meal is sacrificial. Killing and burning an animal on an altar, Augustine says, is a symbolic sacrifice. Properly speaking, a sacrifice is any act by which man seeks union with God. Thus, the eucharistic sacrifice of praise is not a "figurative" sacrifice, but the true sacrifice to which Old Testament sacrifices pointed. This effort to unite with God also has a horizontal, social dimension, so that true sacrifice *includes* mercy, seeking the good of one's neighbor, treating others as better than oneself, self-giving for the sake of others. Similarly, according to Hebrews 10, what removed sin is the true sacrifice to which the animal sacrifices merely symbolized, and that true sacrifice was one of complete submission to the will of God, the sacrifice of the "open ear" (cf. Psalm 40), which took the concrete form of the Bridegroom's self-offering for the sake of the Bride. Thus, when the church *offers herself to God in thanksgiving and praise* and manifests a genuine unity and love in a communal covenantal meal, she *is* demonstrating true sacrifice and in this way ritually proclaims the Lord's death, the supreme act of self-giving *to the Father* for the brethren. This is why

---

[32] Quoted in Max Thurian, *The Eucharistic Memorial* (2 vols.; Ecumenical Studies in Worship, #7–8; trans. J.G. Davies; London: Lutterworth, 1960, 1961) 2.87–88.

the failure to discern the Body—the failure to live in unity with others in the Body and the failure to recognize in the Supper a sign of this corporate unity—is such a damnable perversion of the Supper. A rite performed by a church riven by strife, ambition, and pride does *not* proclaim the Lord's death but only calls down fearful judgment. It may be rightly performed in every ceremonial particular, but it is not the Supper of the one Christ.

III. *Conclusion*

In the preceding pages, I have attempted to break the frame of the zoom lens, but what I have so far substituted is still of the nature of a photograph or, at best, a video: the sacrament as a moving *picture* of the world as it ought to be. But the Eucharist is not played out on a screen in front of the church; it is played out by the church. To stop here would mean perpetuating the dominance of the visual metaphor that I roundly denounced not so many pages ago; to stop here would be to reject the "zoom" while keeping a firm hold on the "lens," albeit a differently focused one. To move forward, I must ask how the repeated practice of the Eucharist not only represents but plays a part in realizing the *shalom* of the kingdom. The next step, which can only be hinted at here, is to engage the ancient question of how the Eucharist makes the church.

Here, the thoughts of some critics of anthropological ritual theory prove useful, if only to help demolish the lens. Talal Asad, among others, has questioned whether ritual theory is justified in bounding off certain actions as "symbolic" or "ritual" actions in contrast to instrumental or pragmatically motivated actions. Through an examination of medieval Christian understandings of ritual, particularly from the Benedictine Rule, he concludes that ritual was not considered a distinct type of activity but was instead one element of a total program of Christian discipline, training, and pedagogy; "symbolic" acts too were thought to have "instrumental" value in forming Christians.[33] In the light of these comments, we can suggest that the Eucharist is one aspect of the church's *paideia*, the formation of the church into the Body of Christ that she is. Though the Eucharist does not bypass the mind and conscious reflection, the effect it has is more in the realm of acquiring a skill than in the realm of learning a new set of facts; the effect is more a matter of "training" than "teaching." At the Supper, we eat bread and drink wine together with thanksgiving not merely to *show* the way things really ought to be but to *practice* the way things really ought to be.

Here above all the categories of anthropology prove radically insufficient, for the church is transformed into the likeness of the glorious kingdom by encountering the Lord who is spirit, who is the express image of the glory, who is, as Origen said, *autobasileia*. This is the "cash value" of the doctrine of the real presence, for it means that the Eucharist does not shape the church and its members by ceremonial manipulation, as if repetition of the rite, by putting words in our mouths and making us go through the motions of ecclesiastical unity, performs a kind of sacred

---

[33] Talal Asad, *Genealogies of Religion: Discipline and Reasons of Power in Christianity and Islam* (Baltimore: Johns Hopkins, 1993), chapter two. Catherine Bell likewise criticizes attempts to define "ritual" as a particular kind of activity or as an aspect of all action. Instead, drawing on Pierre Bourdieu's *Outline of a Theory of Practice*, she focuses on "ritualization," by which she means a strategic "way of acting that is designed and orchestrated to distinguish and privilege what is being done in comparison to other, usually more quotidian, activities." Both Asad and Bell, moreover, emphasize the ways in which ritual inscribes habits on bodies (Bell, *Ritual Theory, Ritual Practice* [New York: Oxford, 1993] 74).

brainwashing. The Eucharist shapes the church because Christ is present at the meal by his Spirit, and therefore the church is, like the apostles (Acts 4:13), changed by communion with her Husband. The Supper makes the church the church because the communion that takes place at the Supper makes the church like Christ. It would be foolish to presume we can explain this communion in anything close to a comprehensive way, but the fact that the encounter takes the specific form of a feast offers hints and clues about the specific ways we are remade into the image of Christ.

With the current situation of the American church in mind, we can say that frequent eating and drinking at the Lord's table will inoculate the church against the Gnosticism of modern Christianity (not to mention trendy spiritualisms) that would reduce religion to a private, inner, purely "spiritual" experience; a church whose central religious rite includes baked goods is being trained in proper dominion over creation and will refuse resurgent nature worship in both its religious and political guises; a church that celebrates a feast of wine is being formed into a joyful community that contests the equation of Christian seriousness with prudishness; a church that celebrates the communal meal is bound into one Body and will resist the corrosive individualism of modern culture that has too often invaded the church; a church that shares bread at the Lord's table is learning the virtues of generosity and humility; a church that proclaims the Lord's sacrificial death in the Supper is exercising itself in self-sacrifice and becoming immune to the lure of self-fulfillment. Not automatically, but in the context of biblical teaching and a robust community life, the skills and virtues practiced at the Lord's table will spill over to fill the whole church with a eucharistic ethos. In short, the Supper exercises the church in the protocols of life in the presence of God. The Supper, then, is not "God's flannel graph" so much as "the church's role-play."

It would be as much an error to imply that the Eucharist exists only as grist for a theology of culture as to suggest that it is an icon or a catalyst for individual meditations on the incarnation or crucifixion. The Eucharist is not merely a "sign" to be examined, dissected, and analyzed but a rite whose enactment disciplines the church in the virtues of Christian living and forms the church and thereby molds the world into something more like the kingdom it signifies. As with music or drama, the interpretation of the Eucharist lies chiefly in its performance, and its performance should fill not only the few minutes of worship but all of life. The operative command in connection with the Supper is not "Reflect on this" but "Do this."

Scripture Index